THERE'S NEVER
BEEN A SHOW LIKE
VEGGIE TALES

THERE'S NEVER BEEN A SHOW LIKE *VEGGIE TALES*

Sacred Messages in a Secular Market

Hillary Warren

ALTAMIRA
P R E S S

A Division of Rowman & Littlefield Publishers, Inc.
Lanham • New York • Toronto • Oxford

ALTAMIRA PRESS
A division of Rowman & Littlefield Publishers, Inc.
A wholly owned subsidiary of The Rowman & Littlefield Publishing Group, Inc.
4501 Forbes Boulevard, Suite 200
Lanham, MD 20706
www.altamirapress.com

PO Box 317
Oxford
OX2 9RU, UK

British Library Cataloguing in Publication Information Available

Library of Congress Cataloging-in-Publication Data

Warren, Hillary, 1968–
  There's never been a show like Veggie Tales : sacred messages in a secular
  market /
  Hillary Warren.
    p. cm.
  Includes bibliographical references and index.
  ISBN 0-7591-0568-5 (cloth : alk. paper) — ISBN 0-7591-0569-3 (pbk. : alk.
  paper)
  1. Big Idea's VeggieTales. 2. Mass media—Religious aspects—Christianity.
  I. Title.

  BV652.95.W37 2005
  246'.7—dc22   2005012234

Printed in the United States of America

♾™ The paper used in this publication meets the minimum requirements of
American National Standard for Information Sciences—Permanence of Paper
for Printed Library Materials, ANSI/NISO Z39.48–1992.

Contents

Acknowledgments

As someone with an academic background in journalism and mass communication, I might easily have felt isolated in a research program in sociology and religion. I am, therefore, most grateful to my family, friends, and colleagues who have encouraged my interests and to organizations who have understood the potential for this research. Primary in this project has been Erik Hanson of AltaMira Press, who first started talking to me about *Veggie Tales* several years ago and realized that dancing vegetables could say something about evangelism and media economics. This project also could not have been completed without the support of Otterbein College's Faculty Development Fund and a Louisville Institute summer stipend. Not only did the money provide important resources, but also their investment gave me the encouragement I needed.

Mark Tolstedt, my former colleague at the University of Wisconsin, Stevens Point, was an early partner in this research. Diane Linger, Stephanie Rezabek, Andrea Clute, and Lauren Cook were invaluable in conducting interviews, transcribing notes, and doing library research. My colleagues in the communication department at Otterbein College, most notably Kerry Strayer, John Weispfenning, and Susan Millsap, listened patiently and avoided mocking me for having an entire bookshelf of stuffed animals, stickers, and children's videos. I am thankful to Stewart

Hoover, Lynn Schofield Clark, Mara Einstein, Joyce Smith, Eric Gormly, Judith Buddenbaum, and Dan Stout for providing me with a research community that has nurtured me since graduate school; this project wouldn't be completed without the work that they have done. The Chestnut Symposium provided pivotal support in my research as well. I am also happy to finally publicly thank Chris Ellison and G. Howard Miller of the University of Texas at Austin for all that they taught me as a doctoral student. Chuck Whitney was my mentor during graduate school and continues to be my most trusted adviser, and for that I am most grateful.

Finally, I am honored to be able to thank and dedicate this book to my husband, Keith Warren, and our son, Anson. Without them, none of this would be worthwhile.

1

Before *The Passion*, There Was *Jonah—A Veggie Tales Movie*

"Wait, kids, which one is that?" Diane called from the kitchen.

Anson, seventeen months, keeps turning off the VCR. Micah, nine, keeps turning it back on. Jesse and Daniel, Micah's older sister and brother, shift around getting settled. No one is listening to Diane in the bustle of getting ready.

Diane's popping popcorn for the movie; it's a special event because the kids have the day off from school.

As the video starts, Micah catches the opening song and says, "Oh, this is my favorite part!"

Diane notices that the vegetables, the characters in the *Veggie Tales* series, lack appendages: "Where are their hands?" She then notes a cross in the opening sequence—one of the few signs that *Veggie Tales* is a Christian video series.

Diane, Daniel, Jesse, and Micah settle in to watch *Jonah— A Veggie Tales Movie*, the feature film produced by the makers of the popular children's video series. *Jonah* traces the story of the prophet Jonah, who fails to fulfill God's command to go to Nineveh and ends up in the belly of a whale—a familiar story, particularly to children in a conservative Christian family such as Diane's.

However, even though this is a movie that Diane hopes will be educational and even inspirational, the kids treat it like all TV. They are up, getting snacks, Micah's playing with a tape measure,

Jesse's playing with Anson, Daniel's laughing at the song about a "message from the Lord," and Anson is taking popcorn from anyone who will offer it. Micah's seen the movie before, and the others tell him not to spoil the good part. Micah repeats the lines that he particularly likes. Anson starts kissing the TV screen, prompting Jesse to pull him back so that others can see.

About a half hour into the show, everyone has finally settled down. Anson's sitting on Daniel's lap, and they all follow Jonah's travails that land him in the belly of the whale. As the angels sing to Jonah in a belly-based concert about second chances, the kids and Diane debate what kind of vegetable the singing angels are: peas? green beans? carrots? No one seems terribly interested in just what they are supposed to be learning from this story, but when Jonah finally gets to Nineveh to fulfill God's commandment and gives the people a second chance, Micah bursts into applause. And Diane reminds her older children, Jesse and Daniel, about the positive message of obeying God and giving second chances.

As the show winds down, Daniel and Jesse have left the room, but Micah keeps dancing to the ending song: "Oh, Jonah was a prophet, ooh, ooh."

Jonah—A Veggie Tales Movie was released in late 2002 to a select number of theaters, with little traditional advertising and without the kind of blockbuster-making publicity that usually accompanies animated children's films released during the holidays. But with buzz in the Christian community and some well-placed promotions, the film grossed $25.6 million (DiOrio, 2003). Of course, to put this in perspective, *Shrek 2* made $104.3 million in its first weekend, but *Shrek 2* is backed by some of the biggest names in Hollywood, not a little company outside Chicago.

Before there was *The Passion*, before there was the Left Behind series and before *Joan of Arcadia*, there was *Veggie Tales*. *Veggie Tales*, a computer-animated video series that tells Bible stories and morality plays, has shown that a Christian message can walk the line between sacred and secular and build a market on both sides (Gilbreath, 2002). It is the Amy Grant of children's video.

Jesus Returns—on DVD

The Passion of the Christ, Mel Gibson's blockbuster on the final hours of Jesus, caught the attention of Hollywood insiders and had them asking "whether the industry has been neglecting large segments of the American audience eager for more religious fare" (Waxman, 2004). Yes and no. Perhaps the Hollywood industry had been neglecting that market, but Hollywood would be outside the ordinary. Programmers at CBS were aware of that market when *Touched by an Angel* was a hit, and Wal-Mart has been aware of that market: that's why it devotes so much shelf space to Christian titles. Perhaps Hollywood was just the last to figure it out.

Following *The Passion,* though, hasn't been easy, and Hollywood is learning that it's not just a matter of putting God in; viewers also want interesting plots. ABC aired *Judas* just after the cultural splash made by Mel Gibson, but it lost to *Everybody Loves Raymond* and *CSI: Miami.* But who'd want to watch a TV movie about Judas anyway? What Gibson did was follow in the footsteps of Christian marketers on the evangelical Protestant side—he went straight to the people in the pews. He also had what makes a lot of movies profitable: high production values and a lot of violence.

Hollywood marketers could also learn something from the Left Behind series, which had sold more than sixty million copies as of the fall of 2004. Its final installment, in which Jesus returns, spurred marketers to have Wal-Mart give away copies of the first chapter, booksellers to buy ads, and 20,000 individuals to volunteer as part of street teams to tell others about the message in *Glorious Appearing* (Kirkpatrick, 2004b). Sales weren't a problem, though, as the latest installment sold out of its first printing of 1.9 million copies even before it was released to bookstores (Kirkpatrick, 2004a).

In fact, CBS, which first aired *Touched by an Angel,* a saccharine series of celestial interventions that found a devoted following, is now the home of *Joan of Arcadia,* a series about a teenage girl who talks to God. Its ratings are below *ER* and *Law & Order,* but it beat *NYPD Blue, The Practice,* and *Malcolm in the Middle* (Strachan, 2004). The God in *Joan* is pretty ambiguous. The viewer doesn't see him or her directly, only through other people, and there's no mention of salvation or Jesus—nothing that would split the market. This is God in the eye of the viewer and the marketer.

Like the God in *Joan of Arcadia,* the God of *Veggie Tales* is unseen, but also personal and friendly, and "He loves you very much," according to Bob the Tomato, a main character in the series. Christian families started paying attention to *Veggie Tales* in the early 1990s, long before *The Passion* and *Joan of Arcadia,* and among evangelical Christians and those with kids looking for values-based videos, *Veggie Tales* has become a staple. But until a few years ago, few had even heard of the series, and I stumbled across it when interviewing Southern Baptists about the Disney boycott.

"Oh, Where Is My Hairbrush . . . Oh, Where Is My Hairbrush?!?"

The pastor at the Southern Baptist church sat across from me. He sang and, while seated, tilted his body and bopped to the right and then the left in an apparent imitation of an animated cucumber. I was incredulous that he, a balding, middle-aged pastor, was singing about a hairbrush; he was incredulous that I hadn't heard of *Veggie Tales.* In 1997 I was working on my dissertation about the Southern Baptist boycott of Disney, and while talking about media use with families in Austin, Texas, I was introduced to the series. By that time, the series had sold two million copies. Two years later, in Stevens Point, Wisconsin, evangelical students stopped by my office to see the new assistant professor with the *Veggie Tales* poster on her wall, but only one of my colleagues had even heard of the series. *Veggie Tales* had now sold three million copies.

I didn't set out to study cartoons. Ever since leaving politics and political reporting to go to graduate school, I've wondered about how people with a particular point of view use media in developing their ideas. Studying families during the Disney boycott taught me a lot about families and television, and what I found most notable was the degree to which they embraced both Christian media and secular media. Parents used objectionable messages in shows such as *Friends* to reinforce their own family's particular moral culture and tended to rely heavily on reruns of *The Waltons* or *Happy Days* as "safe" media. Most families didn't identify much about Christian media or Christian media outlets that interested them—except for *Veggie Tales*.

After my first viewing of "Where's God When I'm Scared?" it was easy to see why I kept hearing about *Veggie Tales*—it was fun, the music was catchy, and the plots were multidimensional with pop culture references. My husband and I found ourselves watching and singing along—and this was three years before we brought our son home from the hospital. We aren't conservative Protestants, and I began meeting others who bought the tapes for whom the religious subtext just wasn't too important. It seemed that anyone with contact with young kids or evangelical Christians knew about the series, but everyone else had never heard of it.

It's true that there's never been a show like *Veggie Tales*. It's religious media that isn't boring, pedantic, or moralistic. It has songs that I actually want to sing with music that has been written in my lifetime. Is it Christian media? Yes, but it doesn't depict Christ or mention salvation. Is it mainstream, secular media? Yes, but it features Bible verses. Big Idea's founder, Phil Vischer, calls the work of Big Idea a "ministry." Does the *Veggie Tales* series lead people to salvation? Children to God? In many ways the series is both the commercial face of Christianity and a Christianized form of media.

Hey Kids! It's Time for *Veggie Tales*!

The video starts with an ad for the Veggie Tales Fan Club, which notes that the series strikes a balance between *Barney*'s sweetness and *Ren and Stimpy*'s sarcasm. The opening reaches out to the audience, without any reference to God or religion, and would make most kids feel right at home with its nod to merchandising at the start of the program.

After the FBI notice, Bob the Tomato tries valiantly offscreen to persuade Larry the Cucumber to come out for the theme song. He's not successful until he reminds Larry that "it's for the kids." After Larry gets Bob to promise that no one will laugh at him, we learn just why Larry's embarrassed—Larry hops out prepared to play the tuba encircling his body. The opening song and dance isn't terribly sophisticated in terms of animation or lyrics, but it's catchy and quickly familiar—critical for children's video. This opening sequence does what the *Blue's Clues* opening does: it reinforces the brand and prepares the viewer for what's next. In this, it's just another video series for kids.

The action typically starts with Bob and Larry addressing the viewer, appropriately enough, from the kitchen counter. This direct address is similar to *Blue's Clues* and other educational children's video, and Larry or the other main character, Junior Asparagus, takes the role of child to the teaching of Bob. From the kitchen counter, the characters introduce the core lesson, usually based on a letter from a fan, and use that letter as a way to demonstrate that what the series is about to teach about God is relevant to daily life.

This mention of God isn't doctrine specific, but references to church and hymns locate the series in the Christian sphere. Bob and Larry take great pains to tell the viewer that this message is immediately applicable, not just for Sunday school, and that fun and humor can also be part of the message. This sets up a tension between sacred and secular worlds that permeates the episode and the entire series and its products.

In the episode "Josh and the Big Wall," this kitchen counter chat is followed by a trip in the imagination to the desert where the Israelites are wandering. Bob makes the connection to Moses and the Israelites with a very demonstrative burning bush pointing the way, but he moves the viewer past the time of Moses to Joshua. In this way the video nods to both regular churchgoers and nonattenders by both making a joke about the burning bush and helping the viewer by not assuming that children will know the history of the Jews in the desert. This technique brings along all of the viewers, knowledgeable and not, and serves to reach both the evangelical and nonchurchgoing market.

Reminding kids that "I'm the narrator," Bob the Tomato connects with kids' ability to understand mediated stories and reinforces his role as a guide. Through his storytelling he leads up to the first song-and-dance number, in which the Israelites celebrate heading to the Promised Land and march off into the distance toward Jericho and into the first "commercial break." This formal cuing is important for kids' understanding of the action in the sequence and is a rhythm that feels comfortable, as it echoes the cuing of other children's media in much the same way that Christian rock uses chords and lyrics that echo mainstream music. Of course, in the hands of writers who bridge *Barney* and *Ren and Stimpy*, it also feels like an ironic nod to Saturday morning cartoons.

This conscious echoing of the attributes of educational video, complete with ironic edges for the adults, demonstrates that the series' creators know their market. Most parents, according to a survey by Common Sense Media, believe that "media negatively affect their children" with vulgarity, inappropriate sexuality, and violence (Henry J. Kaiser Family Foundation, 2003). Parents seem to care less about the amount of time spent watching in favor of concerns over what their kids watch and claim to watch with their children aged two to seven about one-fifth of the time (Henry J. Kaiser Family Foundation, 2003). Programs like *Veggie Tales*, then, hit a home run. It's full of values, not sex and violence, and it has just enough pop culture references and irony to keep adults engaged.

After the "commercial break," which is typically a musical skit featuring Larry, the viewer is transported back to Jericho. This reenactment of the conflict between the inhabitants of Jericho and the Israelites has a definite school-play quality to it, and some of the characters demonstrate a definite lack of acting ability. It feels as though the teacher is offstage feeding lines. The action is portrayed within a framework that is very open with lots of references to popular culture and the Bible and to the series itself, but it's also earnestly educational. Junior Asparagus (who in this episode is playing the child being told the story) breaks into the action by rousing discouraged Israelites who are about to give up and return to slavery in Egypt. Junior's inspirational speech leads to generous applause and a joke about clapping without hands, and then the characters gather round the piano for some traditional church music.

As the Israelites take their positions marching around the city of Jericho in accordance with God's directions, they exhibit a certain multidimensionality and an understanding that viewers would question these directions. The Israelites tell the French Pea guards that "we aren't crazy—our God told us to do this," but the viewer knows that this certainly looks crazy. The marching around the city commences and is moved along by a full New Orleans-jazz version of "When the Saints Go Marching In" until the Israelites complete the mandated ritual. The walls of Jericho fall down and the French Peas scatter.

The viewer is then returned to the kitchen counter, where Bob and Larry make a clear distinction between the Bible story and the *Veggie Tales* version and encourage viewers to check out the story for themselves. This helps to avoid criticism that *Veggie Tales* plays fast and loose with Bible stories and refers kids to the Bible. The episode closes with the nearly standard referral to Qwerty, the computer that displays a Bible verse chosen to illustrate the core point of the episode; the verse for this episode, from 2 Samuel 22:31a, is, "As for God, His way is perfect." This allows Bob and Larry to bring the whole episode back to the opening letter and remind kids that "God made you special and He loves you very much."

A Mix of *Mister Rogers* and *Ren and Stimpy*, According to the Series Creator, Phil Vischer

It's pretty easy to see what's religious in this quick capsule version of the episode, but it's also important to note the commercial aspects of how it's put together, too. By creating an episode that has elements of educational video, *Veggie Tales* reassures moms, the primary purchasers of children's video, that the series will be not only fun, but also educational. Children's video needs to look recognizably like children's video (Abelman, 1995). Children learn the pattern at an early age, and the half-hour format is standard in educational video. Educational media experts tell us that if the format deviates from the standard, children won't follow it and it won't have much impact educationally (Himmelweit, 1996). It probably also won't become a favorite tape in the household.

It's also important to recognize that the *Veggie Tales* series is viewed within a household, within a community. Children's learning of the messages of *Veggie Tales* and the support for such messages and such a series is certainly strongest in the evangelical Christian community, which regards the series as one of its own (Eke, 1995). Eke notes that children's learning from television is built on their knowledge from other parts of life: "If 'social context' is to inform our understanding of televisual learning it should be treated as a site for the production of meaning rather than as a variable" (Eke, 1995). In order for one to really understand the role of the series, one needs to understand the history of the market, the community in which it was developed, and how it now interacts with the Christian and secular culture.

The next chapter demonstrates how tension between the Christian and the commercial isn't really new, but the players have certainly changed. Chapter 2 traces the development of the evangelical Christian message and its search for an audience from the American colonial period to the present. George Whitefield took heat for reaching the masses in an unconventional way, but he did reach them and got a great deal of press coverage doing it. R. Laurence Moore noted this attraction between the sacred and secular in *Selling God,* and the *New York Times* noted the emergence of faith in the workplace in a recent Sunday magazine article. This melding of sacred and secular is also important to note in conjunction with the 2004 presidential election, in which churches played a key role in turning out voters.

Chapter 3 traces the development of the series and the company that created it. *Veggie Tales,* like many successful media products, has a genesis mythology. This one revolves around two guys, a dream, and a computer. But the development of the series and its marketing success also illustrate significant dimensions of both the Christian and mainstream media industry, the ways in which they are competitive with each other, and the ways in which they collaborate with each other. Because this is a book about a media product, not a broadcast or cable program, this allows for exploration of manufacturing, distribution, the impact of Christian bookstores, and the power of Wal-Mart. The theme of the dual market for *Veggie Tales* is fully integrated here, because the series' success outside the Christian bookstore is owed to the retail dominance of Wal-Mart, the demographic makeup of the *Veggie Tales* audience, and story lines that are attractive to those seeking Christian media and those just seeking a good story.

The story itself is paramount in chapter 4. *Veggie Tales'* success is tied to the fun stories, catchy songs, and likable characters. Is it Christian media? Or is it what the viewer (or purchaser) wants it to be? As the series develops and the feature-length film, *Jonah,* is released in 2002, does the series become more secular? What makes media Christian anyway?

Who watches *Veggie Tales,* and why is this audience attractive to merchandisers? Is it the audience or the media that makes the message religious or Christian? The *Veggie Tales* audience finally comes to center screen in chapter 5. Audience members debate the role of the series in the lives of children, religious education, and home-based viewing. What is "safe" media in the eyes of parents, and how has the series fit that ideal? Is the use of the series intentional as a form of moral or religious education, or is it simply an acceptable video pacifier? As one father said, "With four kids, sometimes you just need a little peace." Consciously Christian fans are pretty skeptical of the methods used by Christian media, and some wonder if the series (and other media like it) has gone too far in pursuit of the audience.

Teenage Mutant Ninja Turtles. My Pretty Pony. Bratz. Harry Potter. The core media product of these brands, based in the car toon or book, is only one aspect of the marketing strategy and only one aspect of the profit stream. *Veggie Tales* is no different from other children's media in this respect. Just as Spiderman fans can have a complete ensemble for the bedroom, *Veggie Tales* fans can purchase T-shirts, key chains, bookmarks, books, stuffed animals, and Curad bandages that continue the themes and brands of the video and film products. This merchandising of *Veggie Tales* products isn't limited to Family Christian Stores or Berean but is instead also featured at Toys "R" Us, Wal-Mart, Kmart, Target, Kohl's, ShopKo, Meijer, Sam's Club, and Costco. Chapter 6 delves into the production, distribution, and marketing of the series and the product peripherals that extend the brand, along with the role of mass merchandisers such as Wal-Mart in the success of the series.

The final chapter backs out of the living room and into the economic and public spheres. Does the economic failure of Big Idea and the demise of PAX and the struggle of Focus on the Family mean that American society is becoming more secular and that media consumers are turning away from religious-based programming? On the other hand, one can point to the extraordinary success of the series, separate from the company, the breathtaking sales of the Left Behind series, and the positive critical reviews and commercial success of CBS's *Joan of Arcadia* to see that the marketplace is quite welcoming to religious messages. One reason for this may be that the themes of God, spirituality, and religion offer opportunities for diverse and robust plotlines in a manner similar to the themes that have supported the *Law and Order* franchise and the never-ending *ER* series. Some would say, too, that the uncertainty of the post–September 11 world encourages people to seek refuge in the spiritual and religious dimensions. I would also contend that the demographic nature of the audience for these messages—stable, family-oriented, middle class—is precisely that sought by advertisers, marketers, and merchandisers.

This story, then, like the video series it is about, is not just about religion, or videos, or vegetables; it is about media and religion together and separately, families, children, churches, Wal-Mart, markets, audiences, and economics. It is about a series of videos about little vegetables trying to do the right thing, and about how that series connects a diverse range of audiences and markets.

References

Abelman, R. (1995). Gifted, LD and gifted/LD children's understanding of temporal sequencing on television. *Journal of Broadcasting and Electronic Media*, 39(3), 297–313.

DiOrio, C. (2003, September 3). Classic gets Big Idea. *Variety*, p. 8.

Eke, R. (1995). Context and utterance in the study of children's media learning. *Journal of Educational Television*, 21(2), 101–112.

Gilbreath, E. (2002, October 4). The top tomato. *Christianity Today*.

Henry J. Kaiser Family Foundation. (2003). *Key facts: Parents and media*. Menlo Park, CA: Henry J. Kaiser Family Foundation.

Himmelweit, H. (1996). Children and television. In E. Dennis and E. Wartella (Eds.), *American communication research: The remembered history*, 71–83. Mahwah, NJ: Lawrence Erlbaum.

Kirkpatrick, D. D. (2004a, March 8). Final novel in evangelical Christian series is a best seller before going on sale. *The New York Times*.

———. (2004b, March 29). In 12th book of best-selling series, Jesus returns. *The New York Times*.

Strachan, A. (2004, January 23). Weekly conversations with God are a surprise hit with viewers: Joan of Arcadia is holding its own in a crowded field. *The Vancouver Sun*, p. D8.

Waxman, S. (2004, March 16). 'Passion' has Hollywood seeing more biblical films. *Columbus Dispatch*, p. D7.

2

"There's Never Ever, Ever, Ever, Ever, Ever Been a Show Like *Veggie Tales!*"

Every *Veggie Tales* episode starts with that assertion that there's never been a show like *Veggie Tales*. True? Yes and no. It's true that Big Idea was out in front in computer-generated animation and innovation, and it's certainly true that *Veggie Tales* raised the standards for Christian children's video, but nothing ever like *Veggie Tales*? Within the arena of the home video, yes . . . but one should consider the foundation of Protestant communication and the free market of American religion as well. In that sense, *Veggie Tales* is a logical development and a continuation—but not necessarily something that's never, ever been seen before.

Crossing Over—Colonial Style

In the eighteenth century, revivalists adapted old pieties and sentiments to compete in the religious marketplace of colonial America (Hambrick-Stowe, 1993). The challenge of religious freedom meant that one had to compete for adherents and not simply assume membership by nationality or heritage. The promise of religious freedom meant that religion could compete for new followers and could grow outside prescribed boundaries. However, the subsequent challenge of that competition and change was the risk that doctrine could abandon significant tenets in favor of popularity. This was a risk that many proselytizers were willing to take. Some congregations, certainly, would remain traditional and ritual-laden, while others saw it as a mandate within Christianity to seek those with simpler tastes. "The more degraded the people were, the more they needed to be reached" (Moore, 1994).

Religion Makes News

In the early 1700s, as today, newspapers didn't cover religion unless it intersected notably with war, politics, or other events of the secular world. George Whitefield, an eighteenth-century revivalist transplanted from London, is forgotten by many in the secular world (Stout, 1993), but he laid much of the groundwork for popularizing religion that was built upon by D. L. Moody and Billy Graham. Whitefield used the press as his organizing base, not the church. While this didn't endear him to traditional leaders in organized religion, it did bring attention and converts.

Whitefield understood better than his eighteenth-century contemporaries and probably better than his twenty-first-century heirs that the media "represented the perfect form of public outreach, for it reached precisely the 'customers' who eluded the nets of printed sermons and settled churches" (Stout, 1993). Whitefield made himself an object of news coverage and let that coverage bring listeners. His authority came from his popularity and his press coverage, not from his access to the traditional church hierarchy. While D. L. Moody, the most direct cultural heir of Whitefield, would find himself uncomfortable with the attention paid to his person instead of his message, Whitefield capitalized on that attention in the service of the message.

Another change from traditional proselytizing and recruitment that Whitefield developed, and that is apparent in twentieth-century organizations such as Focus on the Family and *Veggie*

Tales, was the base as the organization, not the church or the denomination. He was popular, but not profound and not theologically based. The audience changed with the meeting; the only constant was Whitefield and his promotions (Stout, 1993). There was no creed, and while this might draw the criticism of purists, it would also avoid the risk of favoring one church over another. Basing his evangelism on personal experience as the core text and his ministry on press promotion, Whitefield could travel light both in the theological and organizational senses. "Entertainment, packaging, and profoundly individual experiences of grace together represented a religious 'product' that could win audiences and support. . . . He was indeed a pied piper, but one of such immense power and influence that evangelical Protestants have marched to his tune ever since" (Stout, 1993).

Coupled with the dawning understanding of the need to compete in the market of American religious pluralism was the Protestant embrace of print. As Martin Marty writes, colonial Puritans saw "themselves as heirs and would-be completes of the Protestant Reformation. They knew the role that printing and literacy had played in Puritanism . . . the whole Protestant movement . . . and that without [printing] the creation of the priesthood of believers could not go forward" (Marty, 1993).

Ministers at the turn of the century saw a future in the 1800s that would be considerably brighter with universal literacy and Bible ownership, which would eliminate religious infighting as a result of agreement on the meanings held in the Bible (Moorhead, 1993). Print, of course, was merely the current embodiment of efficient communication. Embraces of a similar sort would be found around other new communication technologies. Millennialists devoted to print believed as millennialists devoted to the Internet did that if nonbelievers couldn't be converted through communication, at least they could be warned about the return of the Lord through such means (Moorhead, 1993). However, Protestants didn't have a blind faith in the press—the press was powerful and would have to be controlled.

Doing the Lord's Work With Secular Tools

Of course, Bibles and a Whitefield-inspired reliance on press coverage were just one means of communicating the message of salvation. Protestants developed educational materials, tracts, and their own newspapers, making such materials common by 1800 (Moorhead, 1993). As Moorhead reports, nineteenth-century evangelicals analogized the Bible to the sun and the tract to its rays. In this analogy, tract societies used materials to deliver the energy of the sacred text to people. In addition, the warning message of the coming end of the world was shaped by some to fit the need of the medium, and to fit the public's desire for fresh news. For instance, public calls for more specifics in the face of William Miller's warnings about the end of the world lured him, according to Moorhead, to set a date of October 22, 1844, as a means of satisfying readers.

While evangelists had enjoyed great success in harnessing both the press and the messages that are most amenable to a diverse audience, some were concerned about a potentially corrosive role played by the media. The American Tract Society called attention to the potential poison of media without a redemptive message and considered the contest with its competitors to be a war for souls (Nord, 1993). The society planned to fight stories without moral messages with tracts of its own, a strategy notably similar to Big Idea's own critiques of children's media. Thus the society recognized the necessity of being in the market for economic survival, but not of the market, lest its soul is lost.

In addition to the embrace of media and markets (and democracy's faith in the individual) that set the stage for the growth of religious media was the domestication of religious experience. This domestication of religion allowed for private religious worship and experience. Taking religion out of the exclusive purview of the chapel and the church left the worshipper free to find sacred space in a homemade altar or the pages of a religious tract by the bedside. Retreating into the comfort and safety of the home allowed individuals to draw a clearer "distinction between themselves and the world" (Schneider, 1993) and to create a home environment conducive to piety. This sanctified home space was perfectly complemented by written (and eventually broadcast and taped) materials intended for private, home-based consumption.

Razelle Frankl credits urban revivalists with further setting the stage for the "electronic church" (Frankl, 1990, 366). Like Whitefield, Charles Finney wasn't afraid of losing the heart of the evangelical message with plain language and an appealing presentation. Finney also appealed to the emotions in his listeners with simple words from the Bible rather than relying on detailed theological study. This plain speaking built upon the democratized nature of Protestantism, in which clergy aren't a necessary conduit to salvation, and the believer can rely on his or her own discernment to point the way to salvation.

The Religious Free Market Flourishes

While it might seem that the competition, privatization, and democratization of the religious sphere would lead to chaos and a general decline, religion flourished. Further, as R. Laurence Moore notes, "the environment of competition among denominations created by the First Amendment's ban on religious establishment simply accelerated the market rationale" (Moore, 1994).

Moore (1994) found that religious media formed an avenue for the enjoyment of media entertainment without potential harm and a means for churches to recruit new members. The market rationale of churches was accelerated by the First Amendment's ban on religious establishment and encouraged the creation of media as a way of improving "ratings" (Moore, 1994). One example of this new religious media was pulp fiction novels, which, while considered debased, were reformed through the addition of penalties for the immoral characters. Those immoral characters who repented were saved in the end. The creation of religious media allowed devoted nineteenth-century churchgoers to find enjoyment of media acceptable.

By the end of the nineteenth century, conservative Protestants were adept at shaping a message to be both appealing and effective, and they were also able to shape the form of the message to fit the available media. While some certainly expressed concern that the message would be lost in the entertainment of the medium, most thought the opportunity to show the way to salvation was too important to miss. This ability to shape the message for both the media and the audience would be critical and profoundly effective in the coming days of the mass electronic media, as would be demonstrated in radio and television evangelism.

Televangelism

Televangelism, or what used to be called the "electronic church," has come to be known as the programming sponsored by evangelical Christians for the purposes of bringing individuals to salvation (Warren, 2001). Televangelism's form and packaging is a by-product of its creation in the early days of radio, when mainline and evangelical Protestants competed for access to the airwaves in the United States. Radio broadcasters were required to provide free airtime for religious programming as part of fulfilling broadcasters' public service requirements (Finke & Stark, 1992). Broadcasters, though, didn't want to make choices between churches—that would be pretty sticky—so most left it up to the Federal Council of Churches. The council represented twenty-five of the most mainline denominations and crafted policies to protect airtime for its members (Bruce, 1990). This also had the effect of shutting out religious groups that didn't fit the Federal Council of Churches mold, and that included evangelicals and fundamentalists. In addition, the encouraged practice of shared ecumenical services wouldn't sit well with churches that espoused an exclusive way to salvation (Warren, 2001). The monopolization of airtime by the mainlines left the evangelicals in the cold with few options beyond purchasing time.

Protests by evangelicals seeking access to the airwaves only hardened the line of broadcasters, and evangelicals formed the

National Religious Broadcasters (NRB) in 1944 as a response to the difficulties members faced in seeking airtime (Bruce, 1990). The NRB, which is still active today, proved successful as a mechanism for promoting its members and garnering airtime for evangelicals. The on-air preachers evidenced a certain comfort with asking for money from those seeking salvation or those viewers who were already saved (which was more likely). "Televangelists offered viewers the product of salvation, in Hadden's terms, and asked them to contribute in order to help the broadcasts to continue to reach new (and unsaved) viewers" (Hadden, 1993; Warren, 2001).

These challenges, like the challenges faced by evangelists in the colonial period, only taught televangelists how to hone their craft and perfect their skills. Televangelists learned to produce programming that was engaging enough for some to watch daily and urgent enough for some to give money. When the Federal Communications Commission overturned its ruling in 1960 mandating free airtime that had benefited the mainlines, evangelicals were ready to pay for the time that the mainlines were unable to keep for free. In addition, the use of videotape for distribution of programming to stations set the stage for televangelists to create a national "network" of sorts (Roof, 1997). The ability of evangelicals both to pay for time and to harness technology for then innovative means of program distribution made them much more prominent on the airwaves.

While televangelists have captured attention for sex and money scandals and for their access to politicians, what's relevant for this discussion is how they effectively engaged both sacred rhetoric and secular culture and systems. Televangelism, religious services, talk shows, and news programs carried over broadcast or cable capitalized on the use of media and entertainment as a way of winning souls and reinforcing conversion. The success of Billy Graham's crusade ministry and FCC requirements providing radio broadcast time to ministries created both an entertaining message and a "channel" for delivering that message (Silk, 1990). Oral Roberts translated his ministry from the tent to the radio and eventually to television, where he gambled in taking "his program out of the Sunday morning religious ghetto" (Harrell, 1993). Roberts's new program with a singing and variety format dismayed the Christian establishment, who questioned the "animated singing and slithering of the World Action Singers," but ratings estimated that nearly ten million viewers watched the initial program and that viewership continued to climb for several years (Harrell, 1993). Roberts could have been quoting Whitefield when he stated his belief that most of his viewers and most of those who had written letters to him "don't darken the door of a church, don't even know religious terms" (Harrell, 1993). Roberts seemed to think his disregard of the pious was key in his ability to reach the unchurched. Like Whitefield, Roberts was willing to get his name in the papers, and like Big Idea, Roberts was willing to entertain. This innovation would be risky, and, in some ways, tarnishing, but it allowed him to make his mark among evangelists of the twentieth century. While cable television became the home of most televangelism aside from short programming using paid time on broadcast stations, Lowell "Bud" Paxson created a broadcast network that was both faith-filled and profitable. This industry-savvy network tried to program not only religious programs but also those programs that would be "safe" for family and Christian-oriented viewers.

PAX

PAX TV, the seventh-largest American broadcast network, was founded in August 1998 as a renaming of PAX NET, a network formed in 1997 by Paxson Communications Corporation. Paxson Communications Corporation, founded by Lowell "Bud" Paxson, controls PAX TV and is the major shareholder in the corporation, which is also partly owned by the National Broadcasting Corporation (as of this writing). In September 1999 NBC bought a 32 percent stake in the firm for $415 million, and it has an option to take control of the network if the Federal Communications Commission allows it to in subsequent rulings (Securities and Exchange Commission, 2000). In addition to PAX TV, Paxson controls other Christian media holdings, including the

Christian Network and Praise TV, both of which work in collaboration with PAX TV.

PAX TV provides "quality programming with family values, free of excessive violence, free of explicit sex and free of foul language," according to company documents. Within this mission PAX TV broadcasts a combination of hour-long dramas such as *Touched by an Angel*, infomercials, paid religious programming, and, since the NBC merger, repurposed NBC programming. Paxson, both through its other networks and through its in-house production companies, also produces original programming for broadcast on PAX TV. While earlier promotion of the network focused attention on the Christian nature of the programming, current publicity tends to emphasize the "family-friendly" nature of programming on PAX TV, and the other two networks, the Christian Network and Praise TV, carry most of the overtly Christian programming.

Paxson founded PAX NET after the purchase of what became a network of local UHF television stations, occupying the 700 MHz band of the spectrum. These stations became viable as a national cable-carried network because of "must carry" regulations that were reinforced by the Telecommunications Act of 1996 and upheld by the U.S. Supreme Court in *Turner Broadcasting System, Inc. v. FCC* (1997). "Must carry" forced cable operators to carry local broadcast signals and thus made PAX NET available to cable and satellite customers. This must-carry provision also allowed for the centralized management of the network and its ability to sell time to national advertisers.

Paxson Communications Corporation is heavily indebted, most likely as a result of the rapid expansion of its network and the preparations necessary to move PAX TV to the digital standard for electronic media transmission in the coming years as mandated by the FCC (SEC, 2000). The investment by NBC was considered one means for the network to remain operable, but it also potentially diluted the original mission of PAX TV. As part of the agreement with NBC, NBC affiliate sales staffs sell time on local PAX affiliates, thus increasing the efficiency of the local PAX TV affiliate stations. Paxson still controls national programming contracts but does also allow for the broadcast of repurposed NBC programming such as news, some current dramas, and reality-type programming. NBC has agreed that it will not use programming that does not meet the PAX TV standard for "family friendly," and this has meant that late-night NBC programming and certain situation comedies have not been repurposed to PAX TV.

While the relationship between PAX and NBC seemed like a good deal for both networks, NBC's attempts to repurpose programming such as *Will and Grace* rankled some station employees and viewers. In addition, the hopes that PAX would become a full part of NBC were dashed when the network acquired the Spanish-speaking Telemundo network and PAX sued to stop its partner from consummating the deal. Since then, both networks have looked to escape from one another, but PAX has lacked the viewership and the resultant ad revenue to allow Paxson to repurchase full control. Its programming can no longer be identified as Christian or even "family friendly" except in the loosest terms. The latest plan for cooperation between NBC and PAX includes a reality program called *Cold Turkey* (Carter, 2004) in which smokers live together while quitting. The pro-health message is seen as NBC's nod to the pro-social agenda originally espoused by PAX.

PAX can be seen as a cautionary tale for both Christian media producers and the dedicated Christian audience. PAX, in order to keep itself afloat financially, needed to invest heavily in expansion, but that expansion and its resulting debt threatened the viability of the company. PAX's alignment with NBC had the potential to rescue the company financially, but in cooperating on advertising sales and programming, PAX appeared to lose the elements that made it a unique network in terms of its programming.

Christian Media in a Consolidating Media Landscape

Not every collaboration between the Christian media industry and the mainstream media industry ends in estrangement. Some would also question the role that PAX played in the conservative

Protestant community with some of its less religiously oriented programming, but these relationships between sacred messages and secular markets are becoming more common. The nature of the modern communication industry tends to privilege large media companies. The high production costs of quality programming and the desire to recoup those costs through reshaping the same content to fit a variety of forms makes multifaceted conglomerates sensible means of keeping the costs down and the profits in-house. Short of using one corporation to house multiple related organizations, some companies have found that licensing is an effective means of extending a brand into multiple markets. Finally, for at least the electronic media industry, the deregulatory trend has meant that survival of all but the largest of media corporations is in doubt. A network such as PAX really couldn't easily be created from scratch any longer, and the best hope that PAX has is an agreeable relationship with a corporate owner.

These pressures on small media companies, then, make it difficult for small religiously oriented media companies to do well economically and stay within their mission. George Whitefield only needed to feed himself, get up on a soapbox, and pass the hat. Free media was easy to get, and the public didn't expect dancing puppets or high production values. Skating the edge between entertainment and proselytizing meant that one could bring the two audiences together, and there were no advertisers to demand a tightly focused audience demographic. Of course, the ability of and the willingness of Christian evangelists to make messages and media that were attractive and accessible certainly led to the growth of evangelical Christianity. This attractiveness and growth of the market also led this one segment to be viable in the mass media landscape for a number of years, as was demonstrated by the mid-twentieth-century proliferation of televangelism. But as the cost of media production grew and the demands of the market became more sophisticated, it became harder for an independent company to remain a player, and as the media landscape has consolidated, that independence has become nearly impossible. Certainly there are ministries such as Focus on the Family, but a company that needs to profit to survive is going to find the current landscape challenging.

It's true that there's never been a show like *Veggie Tales* and there's never been a company like Big Idea. But it's also true that the message of *Veggie Tales* owes a great deal to the compromises made by early Christian communicators and that the history and future of Big Idea were in many ways shaped by the challenging environment in which it sought to survive. Phil Vischer and his colleagues had a vision that Christian kids' media could be fun and "safe" and profitable. They also had a vision of a Christian company that was as market savvy as any media company could be. Both of those visions came true, but in some ways the success of the idea, the brand, and the marketing savvy made it almost impossible for Big Idea to succeed as an independent company.

References

Bruce, S. (1990). *Pray TV: Televangelism in America*. London: Routledge.

Carter, B. (2004, August 23). NBC Universal and Paxson: An odd dance to a divorce. *The New York Times*.

Finke, R., & Stark, R. (1992). *The churching of America: Winners and losers in our religious economy*. New Brunswick, NJ: Rutgers University Press.

Frankl, R. (1990). A hybrid institution. In R. Abelman and S. M. Hoover (Eds.), *Religious television: Controversies and conclusions*. Norwood, NJ: Ablex.

Hadden, J. (1993). The rise and fall of American televangelism. In C. Roof (Ed.), *Religion in the Nineties*. Newbury Park, CA: Sage.

Hambrick-Stowe, C. E. (1993). The spirit of the old writers. In L. I. Sweet (Ed.), *Communication and change in American religious history*, 126–140. Grand Rapids, MI: Eerdmans.

Harrell, D. E. (1993). Oral Roberts: Religious media pioneer. In L. I. Sweet (Ed.), *Communication and change in American religious history*, 320–334. Grand Rapids, MI: Eerdmans.

Marty, M. E. (1993). Protestantism and capitalism. In L. I. Sweet (Ed.), *Communication and change in American religious history*, 91–107. Grand Rapids, MI: Eerdmans.

McConnell, B. (2001, February 26). Ch. 60–69 occupants band together to demand multiple carriage. *Broadcasting and Cable*.

Moore, R. L. (1994). *Selling God: American religion in the marketplace of culture*. New York: Oxford University Press.

Moorhead, J. H. (1993). The millennium and the media. In L. I. Sweet (Ed.), *Communication and change in American religious history*, 216–238. Grand Rapids, MI: Eerdmans.

Nord, D. P. (1993). Religious publishing and the marketplace. In L. I. Sweet (Ed.), *Communication and change in American religious history*, 239–269. Grand Rapids, MI: Eerdmans.

Roof, C. (1997). Blurred boundaries: Religion and prime time television. In M. Suman (Ed.), *Religion and prime time television*, 61–68. Westport, CT: Praeger.

Schneider, A. G. (1993). From democratization to domestication. In L. I. Sweet (Ed.), *Communication and change in American religious history*, 141–164. Grand Rapids, MI: Eerdmans.

Securities and Exchange Commission. (2000, March 13). 10-K filing of independent audit of Paxson Communications Corporation. Price Waterhouse Coopers LLP. www.sec.gov/Archives/edgar/data/923877/0000950144-00-003149.txt.

Silk, M. (1990). The rise of the "New Evangelicalism": Shock and adjustment. In W. R. Hutchinson (Ed.), *Between the times: The travail of the Protestant establishment in America, 1900–1960*, 278–299. New York: Cambridge University Press.

Stout, H. S. (1993). Religion, communications and the career of George Whitefield. In L. I. Sweet (Ed.), *Communication and change in American religious history*, 481. Grand Rapids, MI: Eerdmans.

Turner Broadcasting System, Inc. v. FCC, 520 U.S. 180 (1997).

Warren, H. (2001). Televangelism. *International encyclopedia of the social and behavioral sciences*, 15,565–15,568. Amsterdam, NY: Elsevier.

3

From the Computer in the Spare Bedroom to the Big Box Store

> Big Idea was founded in a spare bedroom by computer animator and storyteller Phil Vischer in July of 1993. With one computer, little capital and no connections, Phil set out with the goal of creating values-based family media products. . . . The future is looking good for the baby media company that only a few short years ago consisted of one guy in a spare bedroom with almost nothing but a big idea.
>
> —Big Idea Productions, 2003b

Before *Veggie Tales* hit the scene, Christian children's media was mostly "life of Jesus"-type Bible stories, re-creations of classic parables, and gospel sing-alongs. Focus on the Family had been producing kids' media, with its series *Adventures in Odyssey* debuting in audio format in 1987 and video in 1991, but the market otherwise was pretty limited, and the *Odyssey* series was geared for school-age kids.

However, the market for children's media as a whole was poised for a boost as VCRs rapidly became standard home equipment. During the 1980s, home VCR ownership went from 9 percent of households to 90 percent (Dominick, Sherman & Messere, 2000). The adoption cycle for videocassette recorders was truly startling, and it quickly became clear that the recorders would be used for more than recording daytime television to watch at night. Consumers were ready for home video entertainment.

Big Idea Productions started out largely as an enterprise of family and friends. Phil Vischer and Mike Nawrocki had met at St. Paul Bible College (now Crown College). They each developed performance and narrative skills through the campus puppet ministry. Though Vischer didn't stay at St. Paul for long, he and Nawrocki ended up working together again in Chicago and developing computer animation skills when the equipment for production was first being developed in the mid-1980s.

Phil's wife, Lisa, became the voice of Junior Asparagus, and Phil and Mike portrayed Bob and Larry, respectively. The company founders like to point to the early days of the company that existed in Phil's spare bedroom with no money and no distributor. One story repeatedly told in the media deals with a particularly rough time for Phil and Lisa in the early 1990s in which they were down to their last $10 and lacked food for their dog. After Lisa left to buy the dog food, Phil opened an envelope containing a cashier's check for $400 with an anonymous note saying that the donor had been led in prayer to send the money to Phil (Smietana, 2004a).

Similarly, the first video, "Where's God When I'm Scared?" was completed without a contract with a distributor, and the company began sales as a direct-to-consumer relationship until Word Music, based in Nashville, Tennessee, agreed in a 1994 contract to distribute the first two videos, "Where's God When I'm Scared?" and "God Wants Me to Forgive Them?!?" The videos were well received by critics, but sales were dismal until 1996 (Big Idea Productions, 1999a).

During the 1990s, the company's website prominently featured a critique of the commercial media environment for children (Big Idea Productions, 1999c). Dovetailing with the Southern Baptist Convention's boycott of Disney, Big Idea criticized the family *un*friendliness of the major media companies, saying that the companies put improving their stock price ahead of quality in children's media.

To many in Hollywood, your kids are viewed simply as another "exploitable demographic." Thus, we are faced today with an abundance of shows that program to the lowest common denominator—shows that teach our kids how to be more sarcastic, disrespectful and aggressive, shows that teach them how to be better toy buyers and better kick boxers. But very few shows that teach our kids how to be better kids. (Big Idea Productions, 1999c)

This critique of the major corporation was new to the evangelical audience, which had previously embraced unfettered capitalism as a sign of God's blessings. Previous Christian media criticism in the late twentieth century had focused primarily on content, with concerns over sex, sexualized violence, and "un-Christian" messages the areas of greatest concern. But as Big Idea pointed out by saying, "if kids like it, one of these [major] companies either owns it or is actively trying to buy it" (Big Idea Productions, 1999c), the size and concentration of the media was also becoming an area of concern. Southern Baptists found this during the boycott of Disney: in order to be faithful to the boycott, the participating families would have to avoid not only Disney theme parks, but also Capital Cities/ABC, Hollywood Films, Miramax, and McDonald's Happy Meals.

Big Idea also was founded during a time of increasing media specialization and recognition of "niche" audiences. For cable television, this meant an opportunity to lure advertisers with access to a targeted demographic; in video it meant the opportunity to develop a loyal fan base ready to purchase not only media but also peripherals associated with programming. The *My Little Pony* series of the mid-1980s demonstrated how videos could be used not only as a basis for selling programming peripherals such as dolls, but also to target these niche audiences. The video market, because of its use in individual homes as opposed to broadcast or cable television, found that programming could be targeted beyond generic boy-based programming (Seiter, 1995) and could instead target girls, or, in Big Idea's case, target families seeking alternatives to mainstream Saturday morning cartoons.

The First Videos

Big Idea's first two videos, "Where's God When I'm Scared?" and "God Wants Me to Forgive Them?!?" were released to the Christian retail market by Word Music. Word of mouth largely developed the market for the videos, according to Big Idea. Christian Sunday schools, playgroups, homeschoolers, and day-care operations found the series to be reliably "safe"—informal code for not religiously or culturally challenging. In interviews I did with church pastors and members in the late 1990s, *Veggie Tales* was the only series brought up by church members, and one pastor even serenaded me with a song by Larry the Cucumber. With the network of Christian churches and families informally promoting sales, the series' sales topped three million units sold—before being placed on the shelves of mass retailers (Big Idea Productions, 2000).

Veggie Tales was both entirely new and nothing new at all. It broke new ground in terms of Christian children's media. It was watchable. It was fun. The songs were catchy and the plots were multifaceted. It made sophisticated cultural references reminiscent of *The Simpsons* and it made it fun to be Christian. On the other hand, *Veggie Tales* took the same basic challenge of evangelical Christian media—how to create media that is both relevant and meaningful—and used that challenge to straddle the line between sacred and secular. "Where's God When I'm Scared?" (1994) coupled a modern tale of overcoming fear (visions of monsters spurred by scary TV, no less) with a retelling of Daniel and the lion's den in a two-part package. The second video, "God Wants Me to Forgive Them?!?" (1994), continued the cultural references with riffs on *The Grapes of Wrath* and *Gilligan's Island* (repackaged as Larry's Lagoon) with Larry the Cucumber playing the bumbling Gilligan.

Breaking into the Big Time and the Big Box

In March of 1998, Target, Wal-Mart, and Kmart began carrying *Veggie Tales* videos. This marked not only the company's move into the large-scale retail environment, but also recognition that the series was attractive to a wide audience. In addition, the decision of mass-market retailers to stock a series produced by an avowed Christian company demonstrated knowledge that the conservative Christian demographic was a valuable one for retailers. The lucrative nature of the Christian or spiritual demographic has caused increased interest on the part of large publishing houses and retailers, and increased concern among niche Christian booksellers as well as those concerned about the broadening of the term *Christian*.

The Purpose-Driven Life, written by Rick Warren and published by Zondervan, had been on a *New York Times* best-seller list for over a year and occupied a category as undefined as "Christian Living." The estimated $14 million sales of Warren's book reminded major retailers that there was money to be made in the previously ignored niche of religious publishing (Kiesling, 2004). As the director of marketing for Baker Book House, John Sawyer, told *Publishers Weekly*, "When a Christian living book is rivaling sales of the top trade release in some of the big-box stores, it helps to explain the priority being given to top books in this category" (Kiesling, 2004).

The interest in the Left Behind series and in other media such as Mel Gibson's *The Passion of the Christ* also demonstrated to major retailers that there is a market that will support such media. Further, this interest meant that small religious publishing houses, like small religious children's video companies, either had to display remarkable savvy in the face of competition from some of the largest media companies in the world or had to merge with that competition. What happened in religious publishing and bookselling foreshadowed the later development of Big Idea, Inc.

While the Christian bookselling industry has boomed, hundreds of independent Christian booksellers have closed. The boom has meant big bucks for the mass retailers, but little for the small-business Christian stores who can't compete with one-stop-shopping giants. CBA, formerly known as the Christian Booksellers Association, has hired former Wal-Mart executive Don Soderquist to consult on how small retailers can better compete with his former employer (Byrne, 2004). The boom in religion and spirituality sales hasn't been confined to books, either; one in ten Hallmark cards sold is religious, reports the giftware industry (*Retail Watch*, 2004). Further demonstrating the consolidation of the market, Zondervan (owned by Harper-Collins) and Thomas Nelson together control nearly half of the revenue in the Christian living segment of the market (Kiesling, 2004).

One glitch in demonstrating the size of growth in the industry, though, is the split between the mass media and mass retail outlets and the Christian publishing houses and Christian booksellers. Each side keeps its own sales figures and reports as proprietary information, much to the consternation of writers with *Publishers Weekly* and industry members themselves. This lack of consolidation of research has meant that some best-selling titles have been overlooked by the *New York Times* lists, despite the fact that they have become major phenomena in the churches. Perhaps this also explains how *Veggie Tales* remained under the radar for so long. What one writer was able to find, though, was a 30 percent increase in sales of Christian living (this category excludes Bibles and other prayer books) titles for eight months of 2003 (Nelson, 2003)—and that was before *The Passion of the Christ* and the final installment of the Left Behind series. Further adding to the propensity of major retailers to stock Christian titles is the readiness of the audience to buy the books—even in hardcover—and the lack of such titles in public libraries.

While the following for *Veggie Tales* videos was developed through word of mouth and nurtured in church libraries that stocked the videos (frequently church libraries stock more new titles in kidvid than children's religious books), the entry of the series into mass retailers opened doors to the broader audience for children's video. Wal-Mart has been particularly aggressive in catering to both the Christian audience and the audience seeking media of a family-friendly nature. Sales in these categories have been so strong that Wal-Mart welcomed Thomas Nelson, one of the two largest Christian publishing houses, with its own showroom in Bentonville, Arkansas. Thomas Nelson is the only publisher with such a showroom at the Wal-Mart birthplace. As Jerry Park of Thomas Nelson told *Publishers Weekly*, "We built a showcase of what a Christian section should look like in a Wal-Mart, and we'll go in there and merchandise it and bring reps through" (Kiesling, 2004).

Of course, placement in Wal-Mart, Target, Costco, and other retailers meant that these book and video titles were attractive beyond the traditional core and Christian bookseller audience. This has been interpreted as "approachable Christianity" (Kiesling, 2004), Christianity that doesn't exclude, but includes. This meant messages that are encouraging with stories of success and happiness rather than fire and brimstone. *Veggie Tales* was perfectly situated to offer this positive view. *TD Monthly* reported in 2003 that the children's segment led the boom in Christian publishing with more spiritual themes and product licensing.

> In the past, the Christian publishing segment found itself competing against high-profile, intensely marketed entertainment properties for licensees' and retailers' attention, as well as the general market retailer perception that Christian products were a niche category. . . . Mainstream retailers were also often wary of Christian products. But VeggieTales and . . . Jay Jay the Jet Plane [licensed by Tommy Nelson] changed all that. Leaving scripture out of the mix, these tales instead rely on their strong moral values and have shown enormous success in both the general and Christian markets. (Schuit, 2003)

Home School, Sunday School, Vacation Bible School

Within this opening of the general media market to Christian fare, Big Idea sold its one millionth copy of *Veggie Tales* in 1997 (Big Idea Productions, 2001b). The series had expanded during the mid-1990s to include "Josh and the Big Wall"; "The Toy That Saved Christmas"; "Rack, Shack and Benny"; "Larry Boy and the Fib from Outer Space"; "Are You My Neighbor?" and "Dave and the Giant Pickle." The series became known through home-school circles, Sunday School classes, and parents' groups as a series that allowed one to gather the kids, put the tape in the VCR, and walk away. Parents were confident that they wouldn't have to do any awkward explanations of racy scenes or Ouija board sessions.

The series combined contemporary morality plays and modernized Bible stories that put an emphasis on what a child could take away from the story. Echoing the structures and teaching styles of broadcast children's television and educational programming, the videos stuck to a format that was instantly recognizable. Each tale was introduced with why it would be useful for a particular child in a particular scenario, and each video ended by circling back to the lesson of the tale, its application to daily life, and a relevant Bible verse. The Bible verse was displayed on Qwerty, the computer, which appears to be a commentary on this new, non-dusty-paged, non-stodgy, but still biblically based Christianity.

However, Jesus never appeared in the series, and the vast majority of the lessons and verses were drawn from the Hebrew Bible or the Old Testament. Despite its fan base in the evangelical Christian community and its spot on the shelves of Christian bookstores, there was no Christ. While one could certainly theorize on a myriad of reasons why, from an economic standpoint, the absence of Jesus meant that the series was open to a broader audience than the evangelical Christian one, more practically, which vegetable would have been tapped to represent Jesus? The cruciferous ones would have been an obvious choice, but the opportunities for offense would have probably greatly outweighed any benefits. *Veggie Tales* principal Mike Nawrocki told one reporter in 1997, "Don't expect to ever see Jesus portrayed as a vegetable. Some things are too sacred to make light of" (Albach, 1997). But after complaints from Christian parents, the company supposedly changed lyrics in one song to make the words more appealing to its fan base (Albach, 1997).

In 1997, with sales topping 1.5 million videos, the company released its eighth video: "Josh and the Big Wall." The story is a retelling of the fall of Jericho, and *Veggie Tales* characters were familiar enough to fans by then that the dialogue contains insider references to aspects of the series as a whole—such as the lack of hands and feet. On hearing applause from the gathered Veggie

Israelites, one character asks, "How are we clapping?" The company founder, Phil Vischer, was also becoming a media character in his own right as media profiles depicted him as the family-friendly heir to Walt Disney.

> Walt Disney's words hit Phil Vischer hard and fast. They were brash, bold, even arrogant.
> "Will you listen to this?" Vischer called out to his wife.
> "One evening in a mellow mood Walt reflected . . . I am the last of the benevolent monarchs."
> "How could he say that?" Vischer asked, snapping shut a Disney biography. "He's not the last of the benevolent monarchs. I am."
> . . . Is he a Disney wannabe?
> "Noooooo," Vischer said, stroking his bearded chin. "Our missions are similar but not the same. Walt just wanted to make people happy. I want to do more than that—I want to spread God's truth through products that creatively and technically exceed the best Hollywood has to offer." (Tatum, 1997)

Vischer built on the humble beginnings of the company and the series by giving interviews that framed the development of the series as a way of recovering from his parents' divorce and a way to tell kids about God despite the limited financial means of the company. The choice of vegetables was made, according to Vischer and Nawrocki, because they lacked arms and legs, which would have made for complicated animation, and kids might as well learn to like healthful foods.

The competition with Disney, not from an economic perspective but from a cultural one, echoed the concerns about media conglomerates that were bubbling up from other aspects of the evangelical Christian world. The size of Disney and the breadth of its holdings made it less than safe in the eyes of Vischer. "Mickey Mouse is still Disney, but so is ESPN. So are Peter Jennings and Ellen DeGeneres. So is Miramax and controversial films like 'Pulp Fiction' and 'Trainspotting'" (Tatum, 1997). Ironically, the very circumstances that encouraged Disney to grow and diversify also created pressure on Big Idea.

BV and AV

By 1998 Christian retailers were marking time as BV and AV—Before Veggie and After Veggie—an indication of just how substantially the children's video market had changed with *Veggie Tales*. One retailer estimated that Big Idea products accounted for as much as 5 percent of overall sales (Miller, 1998). The series also demonstrated that it had appeal outside its target demographic, as Christian college students held sing-alongs and adults wore Larry the Cucumber T-shirts (a large green T-shirt with eyes and a mouth printed on the chest).

To mark its five-year anniversary of *Veggie Tales* fun, Big Idea issued an official celebratory newsletter. The newsletter, one of several created by the company over the years, featured a letter from Vischer detailing his plan to move the company from a small video production house, over the next twenty years, to "a top-five family media company with a Christian worldview, and to make it the most trusted family media company in the world" (P. Vischer, 1999b). This plan involved bringing in media professionals from a wide range of companies, both Christian and non-Christian, to develop the brand integration and brand image that the company would need to compete outside the Christian bookseller market. While the primary vehicle of Big Idea appeared to remain with computer-generated animation, the brand would be developed across a number of markets. New hires came from Viacom New Media and Microsoft, and another came from Disney. "Diane Teigiser joined us in April to build our consumer products business (toys, clothes, etc.—the fun stuff!). Formerly a senior executive with toymaker Tomy, Diane brought almost 20 years of experience in the toy business" (P. Vischer, 1999b).

Not surprisingly, 1998 also marked the stocking of the first two videos on the shelves of Wal-Mart, Target, and Kmart (Big Idea Productions, 2001b). Ironically, the video "Madame Blueberry" was released the same year—the story of the dissatisfied blueberry who wants too much stuff from the big box store. Big Idea was diversifying, building, and distributing on a scale that was new to the Christian media industry outside of popular music.

Veggieland?

Furthering Vischer's goal of creating a brand on the order of Disney was the plan for a $15 million development in Lombard, Illinois, that would combine office and retail space in a renovated downtown theater (Knapp, 1998). Big Idea asked the city of Lombard for a $1 million subsidy, and the city buzzed with anticipation that the company would revitalize its downtown.

In promoting this plan, Big Idea's Bob Patin told the press that the company planned to produce a television show and a full-length movie and had "more licensing opportunities than we can count" (Knapp, 1998). The Big Idea newsletter promised that by fall of 1999, "Big Idea will move into a two-and-one-half-acre studio complex in Lombard, Illinois, that will include a Big Idea retail store and a restored 1920s movie theater. The development, designed to house up to 350 employees, will be open to the public for daily tours and special events" (Big Idea Productions, 1999b).

The complex in Lombard held the promise of both Disneyland and Focus on the Family's center in Colorado Springs, Colorado, and perhaps the joining of those two organizations was the best way to capture the vision of Big Idea. The complex would be like Disneyland in that it would invite visitors to immerse themselves in the world of *Veggie Tales* with productions, characters, and tours. It would also be like the Focus on the Family Welcome Center, which has reported over a million visitors since 1994 to its Colorado Springs campus (Focus on the Family, 2004). Visitors to the Welcome Center are able to tour props from the Focus on the Family series, watch videos, and observe radio productions. In other ways, the vision of Big Idea seemed to be a marriage of Disney and Focus on the Family: the diversification and profitability of Disney without the adult media, and the child and media focus of the Dr. James Dobson ministry without the politics.

By 1998, Big Idea was poised to marry and profit from the balance between secular media strategies and Christian-friendly media messages. Christian bookstores saw the series as a boon for traffic, and church libraries stocked multiple copies of episodes. *World Magazine*, a news magazine with a "perspective committed to the Bible as the inerrant Word of God" (Davis, 1998), expressed concern about whether "success would compromise content." In Vischer's interview with the magazine, he emphasized that the success of the series was based on guidance from God and his conviction that the company was going in the right direction. Despite the reluctance of any distributor, Christian or otherwise, to pick up the series in its early days, Vischer said that God's endorsement of Vischer's plan "couldn't have been more obvious" (Davis, 1998). Vischer also emphasized that the series hadn't changed with its entry into mass-market retailing and that the ending Bible verse would stay as part of a series intended to push kids toward God.

While he said that the focus of the series would still be to lead kids to God, leading kids to Christ, at least in the evangelical sense, didn't seem to be prominent in Vischer's media interviews. He defended the soft sell in one interview by saying,

> It's like, Bonk! We hit people in the head with a Christian brick and, when it bounces off, we can't understand why it didn't work. Of course, we also used up all our money making that one brick and we can't buy any more air time or tell any more stories because we haven't created a real company that makes money so that we can stay in the game for the long haul. So we throw our brick and quit. . . . What we want is for people to fall in love with our characters and grow up with them. We want to have a lasting impact. (Mattingly, 1998)

Forging ties outside the company was key to developing lasting impact. Vischer had learned that direct sales and limited distribution would amount to throwing only one brick. The first distribution deal with Word Music, a division of Everland, in 1994 got the series into Christian bookstores and into the consciousness of Christian buyers. Big Idea also began advertising in mass-market publications with the message that Veggies were better than mainstream media fare. Lyrick Studios, which distributes *Barney*, also had a deal for distribution in the mainstream market. Sue Bristol of Lyrick called the series "extremely Christian" and said that it was chancy to take the series into the mass market in 1998 because of the message (Miller, 1998).

With the success of the series in both the Christian and mainstream markets, though, one shouldn't be surprised that the series even showed up in supermarkets. The Randalls supermarket chain, based in Houston, along with Kroger, Stop and Shop, and other grocery store chains, was part of Lyrick's distribution strategy, according to *Supermarket News*. Randalls spokeswoman Kathy Luszler told the trade publication, "Sales of *Veggie Tales* are very good at our stores, and we are planning to cross-merchandise it in our produce departments because of the name and the story. For us, it is no surprise that *Veggie Tales* is doing so well. Religious books are the most popular titles in our book category, so it follows that a religious-oriented and entertaining video like *Veggie Tales* would do well also" (Littman, 1998).

Veggie Tales' success across merchandisers was in part based on Vischer's drawing a bright line between being a Christian media company and a media company with a Christian worldview. The mainstream market was seen as unwilling to support a company that was too overtly Christian, so keeping that faith closer to the vest allowed the series to play to the majority of potential purchasers who claimed a belief in God but did not perhaps identify with the kind of evangelicalism of the more overtly Christian media. This distinction that Big Idea made also allowed it to form alliances within and outside the Christian media industry—a relatively new move for the nonmusic wing of the industry.

In the community of fans, however, one Christian radio station in Duluth, Iowa, organized a campaign to restore the Silly Songs with Larry segment to the new videos under production. In a tongue-in-cheek firing of Larry the Cucumber by Archibald Asparagus, Larry was replaced by the gourd Mr. Lunt. WNCB Duluth organized a letter-writing campaign to demand Larry's reinstatement (Hogan-Albach, 1998).

The success of the series wasn't measured just in distribution deals and radio station campaigns, but also in measurable sales. Video industry experts said the series was notable because it had broken into the market without the springboard of television, which was how Elmo, Blue, and Barney had made the transition. In fact, the series reversed that trend, going from video to television with a Christmas program on PAX TV for the holiday season in 1998. The videos also topped video sales charts for twenty-one consecutive weeks and beat out television hits such as *The Magic School Bus* and *Arthur* (Kloehn, 1998).

If the five-year anniversary of the company brought plans for exponential growth, the following years made the first five look slow and methodical. Just a year after Big Idea made big plans for developing a theater and office complex in downtown Lombard, Illinois, Big Idea turned down the $1 million in subsidies and left the city in the lurch. After saying that the company wanted the space because "revenues are growing geometrically," Big Idea now said that the company had outgrown the space before it had even been built (Knapp, 1998, 1999). The company cited unit sales that had more than tripled, a tripling of staff, and a need for triple the space. Big Idea's Chris Meidl said that the company would need more than the 2.5 acres to accommodate plans that now included the possibility of a small hotel and a theme restaurant (Knapp, 1999).

Books, Key Chains, Toys, and Tees

After *Veggie Tales* entered the mainstream retail market, its unit sales in 1998 and 1999 quickly dwarfed previous sales figures, kept the series in top industry sales spots, and prompted media coverage outside the religious press and the religion sections of newspapers. The Associated Press ran a story on the series' growth and the release of music albums and six books along with the sale of other peripheral products such as stuffed toys and lunch boxes (Shelton, 1999). Vischer explained the need for the products as a way to keep kids in the family-friendly *Veggie Tales* world and away from other "negative" media products such as Power Rangers. "That's one of the reasons we're trying to provide a full line of Veggie Tale products such as storybooks and Bob the Tomato dolls. Otherwise, when your kid finishes watching *Veggie Tales* and then turns around and plays with a Power Ranger action figure, he's right back into questionable media again. Our hope is to give parents an opportunity to create a media-safe environment for their kids" (Walker, 1999).

Of course, the expansion into peripheral products was another way to expand the brand, forge connections with other companies involved in licensing, and build a line of merchandise that mirrored the offerings of other media brands such as Elmo or Blue. Vischer was still clear about the desire of the company to encourage kids to connect with God, but he was critical of other Christian media that, while well meaning, "just couldn't compete with the slick stuff churning out of Hollywood" (Walker, 1999). However, Vischer, while identifying himself as an evangelical Christian, was clear that individual salvation was not the projected outcome of *Veggie Tales* viewing. "Someday, if that happens, that would be great, but for now I want everyone in the theater to say, 'I think I should look a little more into God because of what I just saw.' . . . Frankly there are a lot of good Christian videos out there already, and I wasn't called to provide one more. I was called to go head-to-head with Disney on the shelves of the Wal-Marts and the Kmarts of the world" (Walker, 1999).

Big Idea became more consciously opposed to mass media programming for kids, not only in interviews with media, but also in its newsletters and advertising. Ads for the videos in major national publications drew attention to the differences between *Veggie Tales* and more traditional kidvid fare. However, the distinctions made weren't about God (let alone Jesus) for the most part, but instead played on parents' concerns about violence in children's media. In Vischer's letter to fans in the Big Idea newsletter promoting the latest video, an action spoof featuring Larry as a superhero battling a rumor weed, Vischer described an incident in which his daughter was attacked in Sunday school by a six-year-old viewer of Power Ranger commercials. He went on to critique the argument that Power

Rangers teaches teamwork by writing, "With all due respect, the only 'teamwork' kids learn from Power Rangers, in my opinion, is that it's much easer to beat someone up if you work together with your friends" (P. Vischer, 1999a).

By moving the critique of the mass media away from a discussion of God and biblical values and toward the concerns over violence, Vischer effectively broadened the potential audience for *Veggie Tales*. No longer a God-based alternative and no longer just a way to teach morals, instead *Veggie Tales* offered parents media choices that didn't celebrate violence. This is significant in that Christian media criticism tended to focus on the lack of appropriate moral values in media, not on violence. It was media criticism from academics and liberals that tended to focus on violence. By making a critique of mass media based on the violence argument, Big Idea was effectively opening itself to a new market. This reaching out would, presumably, also be more effective because the videos lacked a religious message more specific than "God made you special and He loves you very much."

By the end of 1999, sales of videos for the *Veggie Tales* series had topped eight million units and the phenomenon of the series was becoming known outside the world of Christian media. To be sure, though, Christian retailers were still quite willing to be the base where buyers could get tapes. Christian retailers worked with Big Idea to create an opening-day experience in theaters for the release of "Larry-Boy and the Rumor Weed." More than 350,000 people turned out to see the new video, which sold over a quarter of a million copies in its first month (Big Idea Productions, 2001b).

The split between the mass-market audience and the original marketing targeted at the Christian audience became more apparent as the company developed and prepared for the millennium. In its final issue of 1999, *What's the Big Idea?* opened with a letter from Phil Vischer that challenged parents to limit their children's access to all television, including *Veggie Tales*, and used the stark recommendations from the American Academy of Pediatrics to do so. No TV until two. The more TV kids watch, the greater the likelihood of childhood violence, obesity, and sexual activity. The key message of the letter seemed to be that the goal of Big Idea was to provide an alternative to the largely negative messages available in the mass media (P. Vischer, 1999c). Alternatively, the last article in the magazine, by Phil's wife, Lisa, talked about what parents can do to give Christmas more meaning. Baking a birthday cake for the baby Jesus was one suggestion, and another was to focus on the meaning of giving at Christmas. "Giving requires a giver and a receiver. It can't happen outside the context of relationship. God gave His son; Jesus gave His life; all for the sake of restoring our relationship with God" (L. Vischer, 1999).

By the end of the century, Big Idea had clearly seen what marrying the Christian market to the mass market could do for the company: 1995 sales were 130,000 units; 1998 sales were 5.5 million units (Bartoli, 1999). The difference: videos in Christian bookstores in 1995 and videos in Wal-Mart in 1998. This willingness to cater to the two markets would become more apparent in 2000 with the release of the second Big Idea series, *3-2-1 Penguins!* exclusively to the Christian market.

Big Box to the Big Screen

3-2-1 Penguins! was also, according to Mike Nawrocki, a way to keep in touch with fans as they outgrew the *Veggie Tales* series, and the company was committed to producing both series in addition to developing the spin-off *Larry-Boy* series. The *Larry-Boy* series would use different animation techniques in keeping with traditional cartoons, not more realistic computer animation, according to Vischer (Vischer, 2003). Despite the success of the original *Veggie Tales* series, development of the two additional series, and countless peripheral product licenses for toys, games, and books, the company also forged ahead with its first full-length theatrical release: a *Veggie Tales* rendering of the story of Jonah. The production of *Jonah* would demonstrate which corporate networks Big Idea could construct and depend on throughout each stage of the movie's development and distribution, but it would also significantly tax the company's resources.

In developing the *Veggie Tales* series, starting *3-2-1 Penguins!* and *Larry-Boy*, and creating the feature film *Jonah*, along with the extensive theme products such as toys and books to expand the line, Big Idea came to rely on extensive partnerships both within and without the Christian media industry. This was a departure from traditional structures that had supported Christian media —particularly video. While Christian music had enjoyed crossover success and had demonstrated sales in the mass-retailing sphere that made partnerships attractive to major labels, Christian children's media had remained the purview of ministries and religious publishers. These organizations, of which Focus on the Family was the most prominent, tended to control all aspects of the development, production, and distribution chain, but Big Idea broke that mold and developed relationships across a wide number of companies. While that did threaten changes in the content of the series initially because companies asked *Veggie Tales* creators to drop the references to God and the Bible, the success of the series eventually convinced non-Christian companies that success in the market could come with the God talk—perhaps even because of it.

While Word Music continued as the distributor of the *Veggie Tales* series, Big Idea joined with Chordant, a division of EMI CMG, to distribute the new *3-2-1 Penguins!* series to Christian booksellers. Chordant specialized in distribution to the Christian marketplace nationally and internationally and also provided distribution of Christian music to general retailers. This distribution deal created a bond between Big Idea and the then third-largest recorded-music company in the world (Big Idea Productions, 2001a). Also mirroring Disney's deal with McDonald's, Big Idea created a promotion with Chick-fil-A, the "second largest, quick service chicken restaurant chain," which was founded by S. Truett Cathy, who based his business model on biblical principles, including closed stores on Sundays (CFA Properties, 2004). The promotion included small versions of *Veggie Tales* characters with each Kid's Meal, intended to remind kids that "it's what's inside that counts" (Big Idea Productions, 2001c).

Furthering the partnership-building strategy of the company, Big Idea signed with Zonderkidz, the children's publisher group

of Zondervan, now a subsidiary of HarperCollins, and, by extension, News Corporation, to provide publishing resources for all
Big Idea properties developed by 2001. This relationship was in-
tentionally forged to support the promotions necessary for
Jonah—A Veggie Tales Movie, and the companies reported that they
would begin product releases in the summer before the film's de-
but. In addition to forming these corporate alliances, the company
hired additional staff to maintain current productivity in video
development for *Veggie Tales* and *3-2-1 Penguins!* while allowing
the company to produce its first feature-length film.

Letters to the editor begging local theater owners to order the
film, churches holding special screenings, and networks of evangelicals bringing their friends greeted the release of *Jonah—A
Veggie Tales Movie*. No trailers were shown on television, but the
Veggie Tales fan base chattered about the show for months before
it ever entered theaters. Big Idea developed and released a
Jonah-themed vacation Bible school curriculum during the summer of 2002 and struck a deal with Artisan Entertainment to develop an unusual strategy to push the film. The release strategy
involved opening the film in regions of the United States, specifically the South and the Midwest, where the *Veggie Tales* videos
had sold well and then opening in the traditional bicoastal ven-
ues where the series hadn't been as popular (Bloom, 2002). Big
Idea also limited its licensing of products related to the film to its
existing partners and created promotions with Chick-fil-A and
Zonderkidz, as well as ValuSoft and Talicor for games and interactive properties related to the film (Burgess, 2002).

Despite Big Idea's emphasis in media interviews on keeping
the campaign for *Jonah* modest by traditional Hollywood standards, this type of campaign built on multiple partnerships, media formats, and promotional materials was unheard of among
Christian media ministries and producers. Even Amy Grant,
whose crossover success from the Christian market to the mass
market has been legendary, didn't cross multiple media industries and develop her own line of action figures and fruit snacks.

In addition to the build-up to the fall 2002 release of
Jonah, Big Idea released a two-volume set of reworked, reedited
Veggie Tales videos under the title *Heroes of the Bible* (Big Idea

Productions, 2002). By using new footage of kids' reactions to the stories and selections from previously created productions, the company was able to take advantage of already-created stock through repurposing. Repurposing allows media producers to repackage or reshow material that's already been produced and paid for and resell it to reach additional consumers and audiences. Producers of network television have used this strategy in sitcom episodes in which the characters reminisce about earlier days with flashbacks to earlier episodes. Of course, Big Idea wouldn't be able to sell the same video to someone who already had it, but perhaps someone would want the key Bible stories excerpted in addition, thus making the product "new enough" to generate additional sales.

Big Idea also released the *Larry-Boy* series, the spin-off series that used traditional cel animation rather than the computer-generated animation that was signature work in the *Veggie Tales* videos. In addition, the company's partnership with ValuSoft, a computer game company, allowed for the development of "The Mystery of Veggie Island" and a game related to the *Jonah* movie. Unfortunately, purchasers of the games said the games lacked the depth that they'd come to expect from the interactive game genre and that the main strength of the games was the *Veggie Tales* brand, although some were disappointed that values weren't a major part of the game, according to customer reviews posted on Amazon .com (*Customer Reviews*, 2004).

Big Idea as a company was growing at an enormous rate and building alliances that would carry it through this growth. The core mission of the company hadn't shifted much from the first statements issued by Phil Vischer, but rather than identifying itself as a media company with a Christian worldview, Big Idea broadened this descriptor to Judeo-Christian, which could help in avoiding being pigeonholed as evangelical. Given the rapid development of the brands and the ambitious distribution scope and time frame, this framing of the company would conceivably be helpful. This was particularly true given the company's plans for international distribution (Kemp, 2002).

On the Vine and on the Ropes

As excitement built around the release of *Jonah*, reports began trickling out that the company was laying off employees. *Jonah* opened on October 4, 2002, and earned approximately $6.5 million in its first weekend, but the company laid off thirty employees the week prior, according to *Christianity Today* and other sources (*Times-Picayune*, 2002; Religion News Service, 2002). Some reports claimed that cost overruns from the film were crippling the company and that the company would need to make $20 million to break even on *Jonah*. Religion News Service quoted Vischer as saying that he was cognizant of the risks taken and that "it's not just me risking my life savings and the money I borrowed from my parents. It means that 200 people will have to find a new way to feed their families" (Religion News Service, 2002).

As the success of *Jonah* was chronicled with reviews and stories in the daily press, the troubles of the company were documented in the Christian media. Most notably, *Christianity Today's* Todd Hertz contrasted *Jonah's* earnings of $16 million in its first three weekends of screenings with layoffs and pay cuts for Big Idea employees. Hertz also reported that the employees were asked to sign nondisclosure agreements when leaving the company. Anonymous former staff members were reported as saying that the financing of the film had been done "backwards," and they had felt betrayed that the company they'd thought of as a family, with after-work Bible studies, had been just a company that could lay them off (Hertz, 2002b). Big Idea responded by saying that the opportunity to create *Jonah* was something the company couldn't pass up, and with softer video sales—in fact video sales had been softening industry-wide—the company couldn't keep the staff on until the next film project was in production.

The chief operating officer of Big Idea, Terry Botwick, said the company chose to forgo outside investment as a way of maintaining editorial integrity, which was a strategy that had worked well for the company in the past, but that decision left the company strapped (Hertz, 2002a). Vischer responded to the posting of this story on the *Christianity Today* website three days later, saying that the story by Hertz had presented the company in an "inappropriate light" and calling the layoffs a "correct sizing" (Vischer, 2002).

But the rumblings about trouble kept coming, and one tangible sign came in the form of a lawsuit against Big Idea by its distributor Lyrick Studios. In an "attempt to increase revenue," according to *Christianity Today*, Big Idea had left Lyrick for Warner Home Video (Smietana, 2004a). Lyrick claimed in its lawsuit, filed in the U.S. District Court for the Northern District of Texas, Dallas Division (*Lyrick Studios, Inc. v. Big Idea Productions, Inc.*, 2002), that Big Idea had discussed extensive licensing and distribution arrangements with Lyrick and that Lyrick would become the exclusive licenser in the United States and Canada, with the exception of the "religious market." Lyrick, according to court documents, paid $5 million to seal and extend this agreement for five years beyond 2003, but a contract stipulating this arrangement in 1997 went unsigned. Lyrick claimed that it had attempted to finalize the contract and sued following a phone conversation with Big Idea's Botwick in which Botwick acknowledged that Big Idea had signed with a new distribution company. Lyrick sued first for an injunction to stop the new agreement and for damages estimated at $30 million in addition to interest and fees. The case went to trial, and on April 28, 2003, the jury returned a verdict in favor of Lyrick with a settlement amount set by the judge of over $10.3 million (*Lyrick Studios, Inc. v. Big Idea Productions, Inc.*, 2002); in the words of Vischer, "it was over" (Smietana, 2004a). Big Idea had offered to settle the case for $400,000 (Smietana, 2004a), and attorneys for Lyrick Studios, now HIT Productions, refused to say what or if they ever were paid, but that settlement on the heels of *Jonah* was more than the company could bear.

The $11 million settlement, ongoing staff costs, and the need for plans beyond the immediate future meant that Big Idea would need to seek help. In its more confident days, the company had teamed with another Christian media producer to attempt to purchase Word Records before it was sold to Gaylord

Entertainment (and, subsequently, to Warner Bros.) but had failed to come up with all of the cash needed and had lost money in the attempt (Hertz & Olsen, 2003). But with the lawsuit and the economic changes, along with the potential of a softening video market, on which Vischer himself commented, "the market for half-hour video really doesn't exist anymore" (McCormick & Cox, 1999), Big Idea watchers weren't too surprised that the company was seeking a new business plan. The company's staff was down to 25 percent of its *Jonah* production size. And according to Vischer, sales had been flat since 2000, and by 2003 the company was $40 million in debt, a scenario he described as "falling down a flight of stairs in slow motion" (Smietana, 2004b).

On September 2, 2003, Big Idea filed for bankruptcy. The move was intended to facilitate the sale of the company to Classic Media LLC, which bought the company's assets (including the copyrights for Bob and Larry) for $19.3 million (*San Diego Union Tribune*, 2003). The price of the company was relatively low because the company "had mortgaged its right in multi-year distribution deals in 2001. Rights are due to revert back to Big Idea by 2007" (Amdur, 2003). The sale was completed by the end of the year and *Veggie Tales* videos continued to appear on store shelves with new releases in the spring and summer of 2004. Big Idea issued a very positive press release, saying that, despite the sale, the *Veggie Tales* product would be able to "continue to advance our ministry," according to Vischer. The company also announced that the brand would continue publishing under the Zondervan partnership (Big Idea Productions, 2003a; *Christian Times*, 2003). The Christian media reported at great length about the concern that a non-Christian company, Classic Media, would change the message of *Veggie Tales*. Classic Media also owned properties such as Golden Books and *Rocky and Bullwinkle*, but Word Entertainment, a longtime partner of Big Idea's, also had a contract with Classic Media for CBA (Christian Booksellers Association) distribution (*Christian Times*, 2003). Interestingly, the higher bidder for the company, Wet Cement Productions, another values-based media producer based in Nashville, failed in its attempt to purchase Big Idea, despite offering $300,000 more for the bankrupt company than Classic Media (Comerford, 2003; Underwood, 2004).

Starting Fresh, but Still Familiar

Big Idea started 2004 in a familiar spot: the top of the CBA video charts with "The Ballad of Little Joe." Its books, produced in partnership with Zonderkidz, were selling well, and the tally on *Jonah* receipts topped $25 million. The company was promoting "An Easter Carol" and "A Snoodle's Tale" and preparing to leave its offices in Lombard, Illinois, and move to Nashville, Tennessee, the home of several other Christian media producers. Moving Big Idea to the Nashville area fit within the larger Christian media industry pattern, as Nashville was the home of the Christian music industry and many of Big Idea's corporate partners and, in happier days, executives came from Nashville to Lombard, Illinois. The city seemed quite excited by the announcement as Tennessee governor Phil Bredesen held a press conference to announce the move and greeted Bob and Larry (Gouras, 2004). The *Chattanooga Times Free Press* reported, "*Veggie Tales* already has strong Tennessee ties, with its characters playing a live kids show at Dollywood, Dolly Parton's theme park in Pigeon Forge. Also, distributors such as the EMI Christian Music Group are nearby, and music in the shows and CD was produced in Nashville" (Gouras, 2004).

Most of the original creative staff from *Veggie Tales*, including Mike Nawrocki, would be moving to Nashville, but Vischer stayed behind in the Chicago area to write one new episode a year and children's books.

The series is far from over. Fans still get regular e-mail on new videos, games, and company updates. Some longtime fans debate the merits of the new videos on Amazon.com; they say they can tell the difference and mourn the loss of the original company. But Classic Media seems confident that aside from the purists, the *Veggie Tales* product still has an audience.

References

Albach, S. H. (1997, June 18). Veggie values. *Minneapolis Star Tribune*, p. 1E.

Amdur, M. (2003, October 3). Veggies sale tale. *Variety*, p. 8.

Bartoli, E. (1999, March 17). Produce with an attitude: Veggie Tales videos dish out Christian values with a side order of fun. *The Morning Call* (Allentown, PA).

Big Idea Productions. (1999a). *Company info*. Retrieved April 27, 1999, from www.bigidea.com/company/info.asp.

Big Idea Productions. (1999b). The history. *What's the Big Idea?* p. 23.

Big Idea Productions. (1999c). *Media in the 90's*. Retrieved April 21, 1999, from www.bigidea.com/grownups/articles/mediainthe90s.asp.

Big Idea Productions. (2000). *Company history*. Retrieved November 28, 2000, from www.bigidea.com/company/about/history.htm.

Big Idea Productions. (2001a). *Big Idea signs new deal with Chordant* (press release). Lombard, Illinois.

Big Idea Productions. (2001b). *Our history*. Retrieved December 15, 2003, from www.bigidea.com/company/press/history.htm.

Big Idea Productions. (2001c). *Veggie Tales makes return to Chick-fil-A* (press release). Lombard, Illinois.

Big Idea Productions. (2002). *New "Heroes of the Bible" video collection* (press release). Lombard, Illinois.

Big Idea Productions. (2003a). *Acquisition of Big Idea by Classic Media receives final confirmation* (press release). Lombard, Illinois.

Big Idea Productions. (2003b). *Our story*. Retrieved July 1, 2004, from www.bigidea.com/company/ourstory.htm.

Bloom, D. (2002, September 30–October 6). God is in the details. *Variety*, p. 8.

Burgess, A. (2002, May 1). Veggie Tales nibbles its way to mass market with an upcoming feature film. *Kidscreen*, p. 19.

Byrne, M. (2004, June 30). *Christian retailers balance ministry, savvy in competitive climate*. Retrieved July 6, 2004, from www.beliefnet.com/story/148/story_14853.html.

CFA Properties. (2004). *Biography of S. Truett Cathy*. Retrieved July 21, 2004, from www.chick-fil-a.com/Company.asp.

Christian Times. (2003, October). Big Idea Productions purchased by Classic Media. p. 2.

Comerford, M. (2003, November 1). Cartoon companies want Big Idea, lower bid wins bankrupt "Veggie Tales." *Chicago Daily Herald*, p. 1.

Customer Reviews. (2004). Retrieved July 21, 2004, from www.amazon .com/exec/obidos/tg/detail/-/B00006JK24/qid=1090438746/sr= 8-2/ref=sr_8_xs_ap_i2_xgl65/104-3892220-8420735?v=glance&s= software&n=507846.

Davis, R. (1998, December 12). Veggie Tales, Veggie sales. *World*, p. 13.

Dominick, J. R., Sherman, B. L., & Messere, F. (2000). *Broadcasting, cable, the Internet and beyond*, 4th ed. Boston: McGraw-Hill Higher Education.

Focus on the Family. (2004). *Welcome center*. Retrieved July 15, 2004, from www.family.org/welcome/visit/photos/A0005712.cfm.

Gouras, M. (2004, July 15). Veggie Tales makers leave Chicago for Nashville area. *Chattanooga Times Free Press*, p. 2.

Hertz, T. (2002a). *Big trouble at Big Idea*. Retrieved October 4, 2002, from christianitytoday.com.

Hertz, T. (2002b). *Entertainment: Jonah has boffo box office*. Retrieved July 22, 2004, from www.ctlibrary.com/8744.

Hertz, T., & Olsen, T. (2003). *Weblog: Veggies for sale*. Retrieved July 22, 2004, from www.christianitytoday.com/ct/2003/128/31.0.html.

Hogan-Albach, S. (1998, December 5). Otherworldly unplugged: by popular demand, Veggie Tales restore crooning cucumber. *Star Tribune* (Minneapolis), p. 7B.

Kemp, S. (2002, November 4). Big Idea beefs up international sales. *The Hollywood Reporter*.

Kiesling, A. J. (2004, March 22). Religion publishing's black hole. *Publishers Weekly*, p. S10.

Kloehn, S. (1998, October 2). One cool cucumber: Chicagoan's veggie video venture feeds families hungry for Christian entertainment. *Chicago Tribune*.

Knapp, K. (1998, October 12). A remake for Lombard: Hopes for a downtown revival never jelled; will costly theater rehab do it? *Crain's Chicago Business*.

Knapp, K. (1999, October 11). Big Idea bows out of Lombard theater: Downtown rehab anchor up in air. *Crain's Chicago Business*, p. 6.

Littman, L. (1998, August 31). Religious Veggie Tales sprout in video sections. *Supermarket News*, p. 48.

Lyric Studios, Inc. v. Big Idea Productions, Inc., U.S. District Court— Northern District of Texas (2002).

Mattingly, T. (1998, November 21). Vegetables portray biblical characters, but Jesus is sacred. *The Commercial Appeal*.

McCormick, M., & Cox, K. (1999, February 20). Amid talk of saturation, kid vid strives to stay fresh. *Billboard*, p. 56.

Miller, L. (1998, September 6). Veggies good for Christian retailers. *The Houston Chronicle*, p. 5.

Nelson, M. (2003, November 10). How big is it, redux: measuring the religion publishing industry is still an imprecise art. *Publishers Weekly*. Religion News Service. (2002, October 12). Veggie movie drains parent company.

Retail Watch. (2004). Retrieved July 7, 2004, from www.cgta.org/cgta_retailnews_trend.asp.

San Diego Union Tribune. (2003, November 6). Big Idea productions goes belly up; Veggie Tales lands a new owner.

Schuit, T. (2003, November). Move over, Dr. Seuss: Hot deals and trends in the licensed book market. *TD Monthly*, p. 2.

Seiter, E. (1995). *Sold separately: Parents and children in consumer culture.* New Brunswick, NJ: Rutgers University Press.

Shelton, D. H. (1999, January 15). *Kids eat up Veggie Tales, videos teaching Bible lessons. Associated Press.*

Smietana, B. (2004a, May 14). Running out of miracles. *Christianity Today*, p. 44.

Smietana, B. (2004b, February). Veggie Tales born again. *Christianity Today*, p. 21.

Tatum, C. (1997, December 8). What's the Big Idea? For Phil Vischer, it's Veggie Tales, a series of computer-animated videos that he hopes will make him a Christian Walt Disney. *Chicago Daily Herald*.

Times-Picayune (New Orleans). (2002). Religion Briefs. p. 18.

Underwood, S. (2004). *Family media giant sold to highest bidder?* (press release). Nashville, TN: Wet Cement Productions.

Vischer, L. (1999). Scrooge Prevention. *What's the Big Idea? Christmas 1999*, p. 16.

Vischer, P. (1999a). Bam! *What's the Big Idea?* p. 16.

Vischer, P. (1999b). I'll do it myself. *What's the Big Idea?* p. 23.

Vischer, P. (1999c). TV is good. *What's the Big Idea? Christmas 1999*, p. 16.

Vischer, P. (2002). *Big Idea responds to CT article.* Retrieved October 7, 2002, from christianitytoday.com.

Vischer, P. (2003). *Larry-Boy . . . a cartoon?* Retrieved July 20, 2004, from www.bigidea.com/other/larryboy_letter.htm.

Walker, J. K. (1999). *A veggie of a tale.* Retrieved April 26, 1999, from www.bigidea.com/company/press/veggieofatale_homelife.asp.

4

"The Stuff I Learned in Church Doesn't Seem Like Very Much Fun"

The Message, Meaning, and Marketing of *Veggie Tales* Videos

The *Veggie Tales* series includes story videos, a full-length feature film, *Jonah*, and several compilation tapes featuring clips from episodes and songs. The story videos contain both Bible stories and morality tales in which Bob and Larry guide viewers through biblical and fanciful lands. In keeping with the motto, "Sunday morning values, Saturday morning fun!" the series uses basic structures of children's video with opening sequences, direct address to the audience, and "commercial" breaks that give the shows the feel of educational videos such as *Blue's Clues*. This careful balance between mass-market media structure evocative of traditional cartoons and Nickelodeon with the messages that Christian parents want has been the foundation of the series' success.

As described in the first chapter, the *Veggie Tales* formula for each individual video closely follows typical children's programming. Each episode has the same opening sequence with the song telling viewers that it's time for *Veggie Tales*, and then Bob and Larry welcome viewers from their perch on the kitchen counter. The story that is the focus of each video is usually introduced by way of giving an answer to a question posed in a letter from a fan, although it's never clear whether those fan letters are real or not. Using the stories to respond to letters from "real kids" is one way in which the series makes the stories and, by extension, God's word, relevant to the daily lives of the viewers. The story opens for a short segment, usually capped by a cliffhanger, and is interrupted by a message or a song or a skit that takes the place of the commercial break that children accustomed to commercial television would take for granted. The episode also includes the kinds of transitions that are required for broadcasters of children's programming, such as cues to kids that the program is breaking for a "commercial" interruption and that the break has ended and the program is returning to the story. Whether the writers are aware of the series' use of these legally required transitions as an ironic statement about the differences between commercial kids' television and *Veggie Tales* videos is unclear.

Following the second half of the program, the viewer is returned to the kitchen counter for a closing conversation with Bob and Larry. Bob and Larry recap the episode, apply it to the question posed in the opening letter, and then transition to a Bible verse addressing the question. This Bible verse is displayed on Qwerty the computer—a much more modern way of reading the Bible without all of those dusty pages. This might also be an acknowledgment of the number of Christian youth who have Bible study programs loaded on their personal computers. Lifeway Christian Bookstores offers six different software packages featuring different translations, integrated word processing, and commentaries for just such computer-savvy Christians.

The stories in the video series can be divided into two main categories: morality tales and Bible stories. The morality tales take some topic such as honesty or gratefulness and use that concept to fuel the episode. The first video in the series included both, under the theme of handling fear, and was titled "Where's God When I'm Scared?" It featured a frightened Junior Asparagus who had watched too much scary commercial television. In the first half Junior learns that "God is bigger than the boogie man," and in the second half viewers see the Veggie version of Daniel and the lions' den with conniving chives playing the wise men who plot Daniel's downfall.

Other morality tales that have a biblical basis but aren't versions of Bible stories include Madame Blueberry's tale of learning not to want everything in the store (that looks a lot like Wal-Mart) and "Larry-Boy and the Fib from Outer Space," in which Junior Asparagus learns that little fibs keep growing and growing and growing. The Bible stories represented include "Josh and the Big Wall" (the story of Jericho), "Rack, Shack and Benny" (the story of Shadrach, Meshach, and Abednego), and "Dave and the Giant Pickle" (the story of David and Goliath). As the series has developed, the balance of Bible story to morality tale has remained about even, but the series has become bolder in spoofing secular culture's children's media, such as in the recent "A Snoodle's Tale," which echoes the cadence of Dr. Seuss.

The opening of "Josh and the Big Wall" squarely addresses the challenge taken by the series: to make churchy messages fun.

Bob: Now in church Victor learned that God wants us to be nice to people even when they are not nice to us. But Victor doesn't really feel like doing that—he wants to hit Lewis back—what should Victor do? Should he do it his way or should he do it God's way?

Junior: I know just how you feel, Victor. Sometimes the stuff I learned in church doesn't feel like very much fun. Do you suppose we have a story about that?

Bob: You bet we do. Do you remember about the Israelites?

Junior: Weren't they supposed to be God's chosen people? That's what the Bible says. I bet they always did what God wanted them to do.

Bob: You'd think so, wouldn't you? But, sometimes God's directions didn't make too much sense to them. (Big Idea Productions, 1997a)

In "Josh and the Big Wall," Larry portrays Joshua leading the Israelites to the Promised Land and confronting the city of Jericho. But instead of sticking to the text and a potentially dry retelling, the video treats the viewer to scenes from the Israelites' campfires, team-building activities, and eventual decision to walk around the city as they were told. The French Peas are charged with guarding the city, and they greet their visitors, who have run up against the walls of Jericho.

> *Phillipe:* Did you hear somzing, Jean Claude?
>
> *Jean Claude:* Me oui, Phillipe! I zink zomone has bumped our wall!
>
> [The peas look down from their perch at the top of the wall.]
>
> *Joshua* (played by Larry): Who are you?
>
> *Phillipe:* Who are we? I zink we should ask, who are you?
>
> *Joshua:* Oh, I am Joshua and these are the children of Israel.
>
> *Phillipe:* Hallo children!
>
> *Child of Israel* (played by a gourd): Hi!
>
> *Phillipe:* Eet was nice to meet you, now go away!

The children of Israel, led by Joshua, then proceed to march around the walls of Jericho to the tune of "When the Saints Go Marching In" and brave the pelts of slushy from the French Peas above. This is, of course, a slight departure from the text, but the video still gets the point across while making the tale more engaging than the usual fare from Sunday school. Of course, this is "Sunday morning values, Saturday morning fun!" at its finest. The ability of the series to place the messages from church and the Bible in a new setting of slushies and jazz is precisely why the series works from both an evangelical and an economic perspective. As Cecile Holmes, then-religion reporter for the *Houston Chronicle*, wrote, "The fast-moving videos usually recast Bible stories from a, well, vegetable's perspective. . . . VeggieTales usually have a biblical basis, but their lessons are so universal and low-key that many draw a general audience" (Holmes, 1999).

The object of the series to draw a general audience is easy to see from a marketing and religious perspective as discussed elsewhere, but it's interesting to see, concretely, how this happens within each episode. Beyond the use of silly plot additions such as the slushy-spurting fire hoses and the fish-slappers of Nineveh as featured in *Jonah*, the series also distinguishes itself from other religious video while aligning itself with more secular children's media.

Making Friends with Bob and Larry

Fans of the series talk about how much they like the message, but they also talk about how much they like the characters. Bob, Larry, and Junior Asparagus speak directly to the viewer and engage viewers in joining them for the story to come. This is similar to the address to the viewer that one sees in *Blue's Clues*, in which Joe or Steve asks kids to help him figure out Blue's Clues, or when *Sesame Street* adults make eye contact with the camera as a way of including the child viewer. Further, Joe and Steve, as do Bob and Larry, leave pauses to allow for the viewer to insert him- or herself into the action by supplying what should come next. By doing this, these opportunities for interaction accomplish several goals: first, they encourage parasocial interaction in which viewers form a relationship between themselves and the characters in the program; second, the repetition of the structure of the program allows the viewer to feel comfortable with the series, comfortable enough, even, to help the characters along; and, third, the repetition, direct address, and accessible story lines and language (without arcane biblical references or difficult names like Nebuchadnezzar) make it easier for viewers who aren't regular churchgoers to feel comfortable with the series.

I Am Junior Asparagus

The opening of each program, with the address from Bob and Larry from the kitchen counter with a friendly "Hi, kids!" and a letter from a "real" viewer that is used as a jumping-off point for the episode, both engages the viewer and demonstrates that viewers, just like him- or herself, can have input into the show. Bob and Larry play out other aspects of human-type relationships for the viewer to identify with, such as Bob's giving advice to Larry and Larry's pratfalls as a way of giving Bob the opportunity to provide such guidance. The most child-identified character, however, is Junior Asparagus. This is, in part, because Junior actually is a junior and he lives in a "house" with Ma and Pa Asparagus and makes a lot of the mistakes that kids can make.

The character is critical in the series, because Junior becomes the stand-in for the child in the action and, in doing so, Junior becomes the one who teaches by example about socialization, God, and family. This kind of education is crucial in the development of young children, and in this *Veggie Tales* videos look most like other educational video.

This more subtle conveyance of information is no less useful to children learning about the world than television news. "Children learn about how fathers, mothers and families are to behave from watching television; they also build up expectations of African Americans and other races and ethnic groups" (Grossberg, Wartella, & Whitney, 1998). Importantly, research has shown not only that children learn more informal information but also that they do so even in the absence of formal language (such as Teletubbies) and while viewing with distractions (Fisch, Brown, & Cohen, 1999; Peng, 1995). In fact, children are more likely to pick up on these subtle social cues than they are to absorb more formal plotlines or explicit information.

The importance of this informal information must be emphasized. Much of what children are taught in their early years involves information about how to negotiate the world. Reminding children that the parent is in charge or who they should trust is key to teaching them to be safe and functional in the environment. Many of these lessons center on who is an authority, who is in charge, and who is responsible. This is not meant in the more authoritarian interpretation, but in the sense that teachers, parents, siblings, friends, and strangers are routinely assigned roles in the pecking order of authority. Children also learn very quickly how to distinguish differences. They learn to tell whether items are alike or different, whether people are like the people they know or different from what they know. This sort of learning certainly occurs in life, but it is also echoed in children's television.

Within the context of informal social learning and teaching of difference, one must consider connections between the two and their relationship to media portrayal. In Gunter and McAleer's (1997) research they show that television effectively teaches and emphasizes traditional family structures and gender/authority relations. They also note that television teaches children about appropriate or traditional gender roles (76). As Signorielli (1993) writes, the "storytelling function of television is extremely important because it is through these stories that people learn about the world" (229). Television provides examples of behavior and informs belief in its repeated depiction of the world (Comstock, 1993).

You ARE the Boss of Me

Beyond the trio of Bob, Larry, and Junior, more powerful authority figures are presented. The father, represented by Pa Asparagus, is the main authority figure depicted, although not more important than God or sacred texts. The father has the ability to transmit this greater authority, such as through the scenario in which he tells Junior that God wants Junior to forgive others who had been teasing him. Junior, in different advice-receiving scenarios, might struggle with his father's advice but through further conversation or a dream sequence eventually learns that his father is correct, as in this scene when they discuss who should be invited to Junior's birthday party.

> *Pa Asparagus:* Are you forgetting anyone?
>
> *Junior:* Nope, I don't think so.
>
> *Pa Asparagus:* What about Fernando? I bet he'd like to come.
>
> *Junior:* No not Fernando.

Pa Asparagus: Why not?

Junior: Well he just moved here and he talks kind of funny.

Pa Asparagus: He doesn't talk funny, he just talks different; his family's from another country.

Junior: Yeah, I know, but it still sounds funny.

Pa Asparagus: You know, Junior, God wants us to love everybody not just the people that are like us so we need to accept others the way they are. We can learn a lot from people different from us.

Junior: Yeah, I suppose.

Pa Asparagus: Well you think about it and in the morning we'll talk some more. (Big Idea Productions, 1995a)

The role of the mother (Ma Asparagus) is more complicated. She certainly has the ability to influence Junior, but not other characters, as Pa Asparagus can. Her guidance is also usually contained in nursery songs, such as the one recalled by Junior in the video "Rack, Shack and Benny," or is confined to domestic scenarios like the discussion of bedtime. For additional authority, Ma usually seeks Pa's influence, such as in the video "Larry-Boy and the Fib from Outer Space," when she turns to Pa and asks what to do.

Ma Asparagus: I think what you've been through today [speaking to Junior] is punishment enough. What do you think? [turns toward Pa Asparagus]

Pa Asparagus: I think you're right. Let's just make sure that from now on we get the true story the first time. (Big Idea Productions, 1997b)

Another way in which to compare the relationship of the viewer to the action in the episode is to consider other religious video. There's been ample discussion elsewhere about how *Veggie Tales* compares to other Christian video; it is more fun, it has better songs, it is more willing to be ecumenical and open in its representation. But *Veggie Tales* can also be seen as a foil between

Christian children's video and video for other religious groups, and a foil which illuminates key differences between the Christian tradition and others.

Agent Emes and Alef-Bet Blast Off!

It wasn't until I began looking at other religious children's video that some elements of *Veggie Tales* became clear. *Veggie Tales* looks normal, standard, and usual until it is compared to video for Jewish children. This isn't to say that *Veggie Tales* is abnormal or substandard, but the series is grounded in an overall American Christian culture in which marketing and evangelism are the norm. When one looks at *Agent Emes*, a live-action series about an Orthodox Jewish kid, or at *Alef-Bet Blast Off!* a Muppet-like series with puppets and live actors, though, the differences become stark. *Veggie Tales* assumes little religious knowledge and works hard to make teaching it engaging and attractive to both the churched and the unchurched. Alternatively, the Jewish programs speak almost exclusively to children with Jewish education or, at the very least, Jewish identity. *Agent Emes* makes assumptions that the viewer will understand not only key elements of Orthodox culture, but will also be able to catch subtle jokes about it. *Alef-Bet Blast Off!* tells viewers what's great about being Jewish—but only if you already are. Of course this makes sense given the non-proselytizing nature of modern Judaism, and that is exactly the point. It is in the nature of Christian doctrine to reach out to the nonbeliever or the unchurched, and evangelicals have worked for centuries to shape a message that is attractive and accessible; thus the packaging of *Veggie Tales* is utterly consistent within that philosophy.

Even in the episode on thankfulness, in which Madame Blueberry learns that wanting too much stuff is leading her to unhappiness (ironic, given the shelving of the videos at Wal-Mart), the Veggies go to great effort to explain the relevant Bible passage.

Junior and Pa Asparagus: God listens to our prayers—that's why we say thanks everyday.

Later, Qwerty the computer offers a verse: "He who is greedy for gain troubles his own house" (Proverbs 15:27a).

Bob: Kids, you should remember that if you don't want to be grumpy you should be thankful for what you have. (Big Idea Productions, 1998)

Alternatively, *Alef-Bet Blast Off!* features a series of video clips of Jewish children telling what they like about Hanukkah and a segment on welcoming a Jewish family from the former Soviet Union for Shabbat. However, while the series seems willing to tell non-Jews about Jewish traditions, the real focus is on helping Jewish kids feel good about their Jewish identity—not encouraging non-Jewish kids to try something different.

Veggie Tales: The Amy Grant of Christian Video

Another way of describing the *Veggie Tales* series beyond its willingness to teach is to characterize it as open. The openness of the series allows viewers to find what they want from it. A conservative Christian can pay attention to the discussion of God and the references to the Bible, and a secular viewer can focus on the moral message. This openness or ambiguity effectively broadens the appeal of the videos because conservative Christians won't typically be offended and nonconservatives can easily ignore more religious messages.

In this openness, the series takes a page from the Amy Grant songbook. As Christian music fans and many commercial pop fans know, Amy Grant started as a Christian pop singer and achieved crossover success in the 1980s with songs that allowed listeners to interpret the lyrics in whatever way they found meaningful. Her early recordings in many ways built the Christian pop genre and were nurtured, as was *Veggie Tales*, by the local Christian bookstore. Without national-level advertising, marketing, or placement on commercial radio, word of mouth built early sales and created a platform for Grant's later, more secular music. While Grant's crossover success did earn her accusations of "selling out" and even the removal of some of her albums from some Christian bookstore shelves, this success built an awareness of Christian music in much the same way that *Veggie Tales* built an awareness of Christian video.

It's in the lyrics, though, of Grant's crossover songs that one can see just how this works. For example, in "Find a Way," released in 1985, only one verse contains a direct reference to God and Jesus, but the rest of the song can be seen as an anthem to relying on inner strength and not counting on others. In the chorus, which repeats that "love will find a way" to make changes, only once does the change refer to love outside the physical world. Similarly, *Veggie Tales* stories grounded in the Bible or a morality play make only limited references to God in most of the series, and unlike even "Find a Way," the connection to God is not made through Jesus, which is core to evangelical conservative Christian belief.

Can *Veggie Tales* Be Christian Without Christ?

Just as Christian bookstore owners and some fans debated whether Amy Grant with her crossover success and then her subsequent divorce could still be considered a Christian artist, some viewers of *Veggie Tales* question whether it is Christian video. Others seem unaware of the series' roots and the series' creators' own evangelical Christianity. Still others find the series so Christian as to be off-putting. How can the series be defined, particularly given that it isn't created by a missionary group or ministry and isn't marketed directly to churches or the churched? Even Big Idea doesn't call itself a Christian company, and its new home, Classic Media, is decidedly secular. But Christians consider the series their own and have great pride in the quality of the programs.

Consider then, some of the attributes that define modern conservative Christianity. First, of course, is a belief in a salvation or "born-again" experience through Jesus, which is not evident in the core series, which doesn't depict Jesus. But there are several other core attributes, such as Biblical inerrancy (a belief that everything in the Bible is true), the importance of personal change and conversion, and the necessity to share the Gospel. Without providing a direct call to conversion via a Jesus prayer or an altar call, *Veggie Tales* is able to lay claim to the title of Christian, and not just because the characters say "church" and not "mosque" or "synagogue," and not just because the series started in Christian bookstores. Instead, the foundations of the plots rely on the core attributes of evangelicalism, and it is the evidence of these attributes that presumably creates the resonance felt by Christian viewers.

First, in both the videos based on Bible stories and in the morality plays, the sanctity and authority of the biblical text is clear. Even though the series might play with the details of a Bible story, such as making Goliath a giant pickle or having Larry the Cucumber play Daniel, there is no question about the veracity of the story. The viewer is taken back in time—not in imagination or in legend—to a Veggie-style representation of an actual historical event. The *Veggie Tales* depiction is simply a way of making the story easier for kids to enjoy, but it is not represented as a replacement for the actual Bible verse.

In the feature film, *Jonah*, the viewer is guided through the geography of the Holy Land, and when Jonah lands in the belly of a whale, it's not metaphorical. Instead, there's room for a host of heavenly gyrating gospel singers. The idea that a human could be swallowed by a whale, and joined by friends to do some singing, isn't presented as a flight of fancy. In "Dave and the Giant Pickle" (aka David and Goliath), Bob reminds the viewers of who the Israelites were and of their unique relationship to God through reference to the Bible as the authoritative text.

> *Bob:* The Bible says that the Israelites were God's chosen people. God led them through the desert and whenever they went into battle God was there with them. With God on their side no one could stand against them. (Big Idea Productions, 1996)

As the story is wrapping up, Bob and Larry direct the viewer to the computer, Qwerty, for the relevant Bible passage. Despite the fact that the episode was drawn from a story in the Old Testament the passage displayed is from Matthew 19:26: "With God, all things are possible." This is used as evidence for the viewer that trusting God will provide rewards and that the whole episode was simply about illuminating biblical truths. Nearly every episode begins and ends with a reference to the Bible and an emphasis on how reading the Bible is useful and authoritative in negotiating daily life. Many of the complications experienced by characters in the series are created by failing to trust in God or in God's word, and these complications are alleviated by that trust.

The pivotal point in many of the episodes comes from individual conversion, another tenet of evangelicalism. One example that is as flashy in the Bible as it is in the series is depicted in "Rack, Shack and Benny." In this episode Rack, Shack, and Benny (played by Bob, Larry, and Junior Asparagus) refuse to bow down to the bunny (rhymes with *money*) that has been responsible for the chocolate bunny company's success. As in the story of Shadrach, Meshach, and Abednego, the company president (or king), incensed that his false idol is not being worshipped, throws the workers into the fiery furnace. But when Nebby K. Nezzer sees that the workers aren't burned up but instead are protected by God, he calls them out of the furnace and is converted on the spot.

Similarly, Junior Asparagus experiences many "teachable moments" that result in his doing what his father (Father?) wants. When Junior Asparagus lies about breaking a plate and that lie results in the potential destruction of the world by the Fib from Outer Space, he experiences a dramatic conversion through seeing the destruction created by the Fib and the impotence of superhero Larry-Boy to stop it. Junior Asparagus comes forward, tells the truth, and apologizes, expecting to be punished, but is only reminded of the lesson during the final segment with Qwerty.

Bob: Well, it's time to talk about what we learned today.

[Song: It's time to talk about what we've learned today, God has a lot to say in his book. You see God's word is for everyone and now that our song is done, let's take a look.]

Qwerty: The truth will set you free. John 8:32b

Bob: You see, the only way for us really to be free is for us to do what God wants us to and God wants us to tell the truth. You might still get punished but facing your parents is a lot better than getting stuck in a big lie.

The third attribute is the belief in the necessity of sharing the Gospel. One way in which this is evident is in the series itself, which is a mechanism for broadening knowledge about the Bible and religious beliefs. Further, although most of the series is grounded in the Hebrew Bible or Old Testament, Qwerty regularly provides a reference to the Gospels. However, the series frequently encourages viewers, no matter how young, to show others a better path. In this, the role of Junior as the child stand-in is significant. Junior Asparagus commonly calls upon the others to follow his lead and does it in a way that is more personally compelling than Bob's bossiness.

Again, in "Rack, Shack and Benny," Junior asks his friends to join him in following a parent's advice.

Junior: Guys! Don't you remember what our parents taught us? We shouldn't eat too much candy because it's not good for us.

Bob: Junior, but our parents aren't here right now.

Junior: I keep thinking of the song my mother used to sing to me. "Think of me everyday, remember what I say, if you will think of me, I'll be with you." I know our parents aren't here right now, but we should still do what they say. Even if our parents aren't here to help us do what's right, if we do that, it's kind of like they are!

Bob: [spits out candy and sniffles] Okay, no more candy.

Larry: [spits out candy] Yeah, I'm doing it for my mom! (Big Idea Productions, 1995b)

Junior Asparagus also leads others to the correct path in "Lyle the Kindly Viking" as the littlest Viking, who works to right the wrongs of others and ultimately guides them to do right themselves. In "Are You My Neighbor?" Junior Asparagus (playing the Good Samaritan) is able to effect a conversion just by being his own loving self. The selfishness of others is exposed by Junior's willingness to save a citizen of a different city, and this example changes both communities. Finally, in the Jonah-related games and materials for Christian families released to coincide with the roll-out of the feature film, Jonah (portrayed by Pa Asparagus) reminds the reader that "God entrusted me with his message for the Ninevites. After all, I was a prophet! It was my job to tell those nasty fish-slappers to stop being so mean! But did I listen? No! I ran and I ran until I ended up in the belly of a big fish. I must confess that it is truly important to remember that God counts on us (you and me) to spread his message of love to others. After all, if we don't do it, who will?" (Big Idea Productions, 2002, 144).

Reaching out to others, the core of evangelicalism, relies on a receptive audience. How does the audience see *Veggie Tales*, and does its message call them to action or faithfulness beyond fandom?

References

Big Idea Productions. (1995a). Are you my neighbor? [Videocassette]. Chicago: Big Idea Productions.

Big Idea Productions. (1995b). Rack, Shack and Benny. [Videocassette]. Nashville, TN: Everland Entertainment.

Big Idea Productions. (1996). Dave and the giant pickle. [Videocassette]. Nashville: Everland Entertainment.

Big Idea Productions. (1997a). Josh and the big wall. [Videocassette]. Nashville, TN: Everland Entertainment.

Big Idea Productions. (1997b). Larry-Boy and the fib from outer space. [Videocassette]. Nashville, TN: Everland Entertainment.

Big Idea Productions. (1998). Madame Blueberry. [Videocassette]. Chicago: Word.

Big Idea Productions. (2002). *A very veggie family adventure!* Grand Rapids, MI: Zonderkidz.

Comstock, G. (1993). The medium and the society: The role of television in American life. In G. L. Berry & J. K. Asamen (Eds.), *Children and television: Images in a changing sociocultural world,* 117–131. Newbury Park, CA: Sage.

Fisch, S. M., Brown, S. K., & Cohen, D. I. (1999). *Young children's comprehension of television: The role of visual information and intonation.* Paper presented at the Society for Research in Child Development, Albuquerque, NM.

Grossberg, L., Wartella, E., & Whitney, D. C. (1998). *Mediamaking: Mass media in a popular culture.* Thousand Oaks, CA: Sage.

Gunter, B., & McAleer, J. (1997). *Children and television.* London: Routledge.

Holmes, C. S. (1999, July 31). VeggieTales: Animated Christian series growing fast. *Houston Chronicle.*

Peng, D. (1995). Children's attention to and comprehension of explicit versus implicit information on television. *Journal of Educational Television 21,* 71–83.

Signorielli, N. (1993). Television, the portrayal of women and children's attitudes. In G. L. Berry & J. K. Asamen (Eds.), *Children and television: Images in a changing sociocultural world.* Newbury Park, CA: Sage.

5

Keeping Kids Safe and Close to God: Responses From the *Veggie Tales* Audience

When working on an earlier project about Southern Baptist families and the Disney boycott in 1998, I found that most families paid little attention to Christian bookstores and Christian media organizations, but they still seemed knowledgeable about the media choices out there. Of course, Christian radio plays a big role in promoting Christian musical artists, and some families are on the mailing list of Focus on the Family, but most families claimed to have never darkened the door of a Christian bookstore.

Most, though, knew all about *Veggie Tales*, despite the fact that the series lacked a spot on Saturday morning cartoons or on Nickelodeon. Word of mouth carried information about media choices from one family to another. Several parents discussed how they would sometimes talk about media choices and child-rearing issues with other parents both in and out of church. Parents who were involved in planning youth activities obviously had more opportunity for these discussions. "We do it [talk about media] a lot with the people we teach Sunday School with because of the youth and the issues they are involved with. We all feel pretty similar that society is putting a lot of pressure on youth these days" (Warren, 1998, 189).

Unlike earlier research on evangelical Christians and mainstream and Christian media, mothers didn't talk about shielding their children from the media or teaching their children to interpret certain messages within the scope of the family's moral code. Much of the audience research published now focuses on resistance to audience messages and the reinterpretation of those messages according to the encoding/decoding theories of Stuart Hall (Scott, 2003).

More recent research on religious audiences for mainstream media finds a conservative/liberal divide in terms of program preferences, interpretations, and approval of programming. This echoes research from other disciplines, such as sociology, history, and economics, that finds this divide emerging in terms of both sociological indicators such as church attendance and growth and political behavior (Wuthnow, 1988). Through media, religious audiences seek to position themselves relative to the larger society. Linderman writes that in making sense of religion in television "the study of how audiences understand and use the flow of messages in the mass media becomes, in part, a study of how people establish their general worldviews and ultimate values" (Linderman, 1997).

To demonstrate this split in the audience for media as it relates to adherence to a particular faith, in separate studies of mainstream Protestants and members of the Religious Society of Friends (Quakers), Buddenbaum (1996) found that mainline Protestants were more interested in educating members about the media than in censoring the media. Mainline Protestants, according to Buddenbaum, also saw multiple voices as key to diluting the impact of negative media messages (Buddenbaum, 1996). Quakers used media critically as an information source but preferred elite and national media outlets to local media. Religious liberals, mainline members, and Catholics preferred more "cosmopolitan" coverage of issues in regard to religion pages, and conservatives preferred more localized religion coverage (Buddenbaum & Hoover, 1996). It is important, however, to draw a distinction between a true "marketplace of ideas" and the attitude adopted toward media education by, for example, the Catholic Church. While the church may endorse the concept and the ultimate beneficial intent of a "classical liberal doctrine of free expression," Jelen writes, "Catholic doctrine regards human reason as readily corruptible, and, therefore, a suspect, if necessary, means by which the faithful can discern truth. By virtue of its special status with Christ, the church seeks to provide guidance for people attempting to make intelligent and moral choices about the information and media to which they pay attention" (Jelen, 1996, 48–49).

Similarly, the Mormon church sees its responsibility, particularly given its doctrine of latter-day revelation, as a guide to encourage appropriate and wholesome media use (Stout, 1996, 92). While encouraging Mormon families to read books that will be thought-provoking and of broad interest, the church also discourages the viewing of R-rated films and seems to be heading toward a more rule-based approach toward the media as church leaders feel more threatened by the media, according to Stout (1996, 94–96).

As the distinction made by the Mormon church regarding the type of media and its potential for concern suggests, preference for specific types of media also seems to be influenced by type and degree of religiosity. Buddenbaum (1996) found that conservatives, regardless of denomination, use newspapers less than other media and trust them less than mainline or liberal adherents. More frequent church attendance was associated with less tolerance, and those who were less tolerant tended to use television and mistrust newspapers (Rimmer, 1996). Those who tended to be more tolerant of civil liberties tended to prefer newspapers. Fundamentalists who were not interested in challenging their faith tended to choose media messages that would support their faith and to reject challenging messages (McFarland & Warren, 1992). In regard to program preference, religious conservatives avoided sexually oriented programs more than religious liberals, and religious liberals avoided violent programs more than religious conservatives (Hamilton & Rubin, 1992).

It is interesting, however, that the same religious conservatives who have organized against television and film in terms of individual programs and the media itself are also those groups who prefer it over newspapers. Religious conservatives tend not to avoid that media to which they are opposed, and, as Hoover has demonstrated, they don't appear to embrace the Christian media either (Hoover, 1990). In fact, fundamentalists and evangelical Christians ranked higher than any other denomination in considering newspapers "not at all" trustworthy (Buddenbaum, 1996, 126). In a study that is quite pertinent to this one because of the similarities in child-rearing philosophy between conservative Protestant and Mormon families, Valenti and Stout (1996) found that despite encouragement from the church to avoid television and the mothers' own feelings about television, 39 percent of Mormon mothers reported that they used television "5 or more hours per day 5 or more days per week. Another 40% were considered medium users, defined as watching television 2 to 4 hours per day and 2 to 4 days per week" (190). Despite what were defined as high levels of viewing, the Mormon women were nearly split on whether television was important to them and whether children are better off without TV. Sixty percent of them did report guilt about watching TV (Valenti & Stout, 1996). It is also important to note that the majority of women participating were home either all or part of the day, and many were involved in caring for young children who may have been the primary television audience.

In the previous study and in a subsequent study also by Valenti and Stout (1996), the authors point out the independence of Mormon church members in making media decisions. The Mormon church is particularly active in guiding its members' media use; it might be expected that members would be more likely to adhere to these teachings. It is interesting, then, that in the study of Mormon mothers, the women were quite aware of the church's teachings on media and felt some guilt about their media use, and yet maintained a steady media diet. In their subsequent study of Mormon women's and Brigham Young University students' media choices, Valenti and Stout found that a group of traditionalists and independents emerged, and the independents relied more on peer groups for media information than the church. However, a more rule-based, church-reliant approach to media choices tended to be aligned with older women in the study—which confounds some of the results of the earlier study. Despite their contradictions, the Valenti and Stout studies raise important questions for the study of conservative Protestants because of similar values and political stances.

Perhaps one reason why conservative religious audiences continue to use the media they criticize is that media have become ubiquitous and, in some ways, unavoidable. Media are occupying the central socializing role that used to be reserved for religion alone. Bendroth (1996) writes in a discussion of fundamentalism and media from 1930 to 1990 that fundamentalism previously "helped people negotiate temptations and provided clear guideposts" for those wishing to live according to fundamentalist values. Media were simply a temptation, not a primary means of cultural communication. For fundamentalists, media are no longer simply a detour—the media are unavoidable (Bendroth, 1996). The central role of the media, then, places it as a site of cultural struggle. Lindlof (1996) writes in a study of the debate over the film *The Last Temptation of Christ* that the release of the film was yet another skirmish in a "culture war" between those who see one explanation for the way things are and those who see multiple interpretations.

> For the opponents of "The Last Temptation of Christ," the meaning of the film was in its effect, a dangerous intervention in a world alive with eternal and transcendent forces of love, judgment, and evil. For those who wrote against the film, there can be only one meaning for everything. This meaning is recognized and acted on in its relation to the codes given in their Scriptures and the community of believers who make those codes literal in their lives. To be faced with a text that goes against their codes is to *dislocate the community* and arouse its passion (Lindlof, 1996).

Scholars in the area of religion, media, and culture have repeatedly called for the incorporation of religion into the study of culture on the grounds that religion does connect people to larger elements in society and provides a means of transition between public and private. Hoover and Venturelli (1996) write, "It is our view that the status of religion within contemporary mediated discourse has strong implications for the broader question of public moral discourse, and the fact of the eclipse of the religious is indicative of a further eclipse, focusing on a morality, community, and broader public purpose" (Hoover & Venturelli, 1996, 260). Wade Clark Roof also writes that mainstream media programming provides opportunities for religious audiences to "find expression in secular programming. The media encourage a sense of personal identity that is reflexive, that is a conception of self as constructed and seemingly more open and protean" (Roof, 1997, 65). Others argue that religion is in itself a bridge between public and private.

Colleen McDannell's (1995) book on religious material culture beautifully and persuasively describes how "lay men and women successfully integrate religious concerns, popular culture, and profit making" (269). She cites the influence of the "Jesus people" movement of the 1960s and 1970s in which followers "sought to experience the reality of Jesus outside of an institutionalized church structure" (McDannell, 1995, 247). Christian manufacturers sought to fill (and capitalize on) this need with popular books such as *The Total Woman* (Morgan, 1973), bumper stickers, and religious plaques (248).

Profit making aside, specialized media "mirrors a process whereby groups formerly dependent upon face-to-face contact are organized into groups by providing collective symbols that transcend space, time, and culture" (Carey, 1997). Carey continues in saying that these media "consolidate and stabilize for the reader his identity and the reality of the group" (1997, 131).

The overall cultural studies tradition of audience research has focused on audience interpretation—how people make sense of the media they see. In much of my own research this has taken the form of studies on audiences who are against most of the mainstream media messages available today—Christian critiques of Disney or sitcoms. Others, most notably Lynn Schofield Clark, have used media as a way of helping study participants tap into spiritual topics, such as in her work on fans of *Buffy the Vampire Slayer* (Clark, 2003). Other, non-religion-oriented audience research has looked at fans of romance novels (Radway, 1991) or television shows. What I found with fans of *Veggie Tales* is, in some ways, a blend of the two. It was interesting to hear from people so enthusiastic about media, a rarity these days, despite the increasing use of most forms of media, but the forms that fans' enthusiasm took were also quite telling in terms of the role that *Veggie Tales* plays as a bridge between the mainstream and Christian media worlds.

There were three main groups of *Veggie Tales* fans included in the study. I was included in a *Veggie Tales* viewing night held in a college student's apartment near a major state university campus with an active Campus Crusade for Christ chapter. The students agreed, in exchange for pizza and soda, to spend time talking with me and my assistant about the series—I'd hoped for about an hour of conversation, but I was fortunate enough to be treated to four hours of a probing analysis of the series and the Christian media industry. Two networks of mothers in two central Ohio cities were also included. One network was made up of mothers who were all patrons of a local children's bookstore (not a Christian bookstore), and, for the most part, they were sometime churchgoers but didn't identify themselves as evangelical or born-again Christians. The mothers in the other network were contacted through a nondenominational conservative evangelical church and a homeschooler's network in which they were active. In the cases of both networks of mothers, they were interviewed by informants within their own communities who worked with me on setting up the dialogues, and I think the results demonstrate far richer insights than I might have achieved as an outsider. In all, over forty individuals were interviewed. More participants identified themselves as "born-again" than not, and the income and education range went from a year or two of college to a postgraduate teaching credential. Income levels and work histories were similarly varied, and a fair number of the mothers worked at home to raise young children.

Why talk to college students and mothers? College students, I've found, are a surprisingly loyal fan base for *Veggie Tales*. The news media has documented the popularity of *Veggie Tales* among teens and young adults (Baranick, 1997; Shrewsbury, 1998), and it's interesting to talk to people who've chosen the tapes for their own enjoyment—not for the purposes of educating or entertaining others, as the mothers did. The college students interviewed in this study provided remarkably frank information that offered insights as to how they see their own challenges as Christians in society and how those challenges appear to create a lens through which they assess the dedication of others.

As for the mothers, research that engages parents in discussion of why they make certain media choices is illuminating not from a factual perspective, but from a perspective of how parents choose to see themselves as parents and as Christians. The use of discussions about media as a way of getting parents to talk about culture has also been borne out as a useful technique by Hoover, Clark, and Alters (Hoover, Clark, & Alters, 2004). In addition, research on VCR use in the home has found that mothers are the primary source of assistance with all aspects of video viewing, regardless of whether the mothers worked outside the home or whether fathers were present (Krendl & Clark, 1993). Krendl and Clark found that mothers assumed responsibility not only for technological assistance, but also for the viewing choices that were available to their children.

> They also were more likely to co-view and interact with the children while viewing. In addition, mothers were more likely to be involved with other household tasks and chores while viewing—ironing, cleaning, cooking and feeding the children. The responsibility of monitoring the children's use of television and its associated technologies seemed a kind of extension of these domestic and care-giving responsibilities. That is, television appeared to be part of the mother's domestic domain. . . . In each case, the mother served as the moral guardian of television in the home. (Krendl & Clark, 1993)

Despite the media coverage of the series and the availability of the tapes for my own viewing, I had questions that only *Veggie Tales* fans could answer. From an economic standpoint, how do fans become fans? How do they hear about the series? Why do they continue to watch it? What is it about this series, as opposed to other options, that keeps them coming back for more? What does viewing the series mean to them? What does the existence of the series mean for evangelical Christians? Is it a good thing or a bad thing that the series is so successful? Frequently when one interviews people about media choices, most of the interviewees go to great lengths to criticize the media and distance themselves from it; this is particularly true of evangelical Christians. What would it mean for them to be enthusiastic about a media option?

The Spread of Audience Awareness About *Veggie Tales*

By the late 1990s Christian youth groups (and not just four-year-olds) were singing *Veggie Tales* songs. The Thursday night meetings of Campus Crusade for Christ on many college campuses viewed the tapes as part of the program, and fans had created over fifty websites (*Campus Life*, 1998). Teens reported singing the songs. Christian bookstores found that adult sizes of the Bob and Larry T-shirts sold out before the kid sizes did. Just as the pastor sang the "Hairbrush Song" to me in 1998, telling me I just had to get a copy, parent-to-parent contact was critical in developing the audience for the series.

In interviews conducted with fans of the series we found that nearly all of the mothers who purchased or rented tapes did so based on a recommendation from a friend or family member. Not one saw an ad and few walked into the store and decided to make the purchase. For those who bought in the store, the store's playing the music from the series was critical in the decision to purchase and critical in the fans' continued interest in the series. The word-of-mouth networking, though, was obviously important to the series' popularity, a fact celebrated by Big Idea itself as a sign of the quality of its product.

Even the college students interviewed reported that they started watching because their friends in the dorms were watching, and one even reported a friend's "becoming a Christian" after watching *Veggie Tales* with a group in a dorm room. The college students didn't think that the series was too young for them or that they would outgrow the series. "I have no maturity standards. I go to a lot of Christian concerts and people would be wearing all red shirts with the face [the Bob the Tomato shirt] and I would ask them about it. So that's how I found them."

Some students reported seeing *Veggie Tales* for the first time at home with their mothers, and mothers are certainly key in bringing the tapes into the home. In our interviews we found that mothers (and grandmothers) would tell each other about the series, share tapes, and even give the tapes as not-so-subtle hints to family and friends. Mothers of Preschoolers (MOPs), an organization to support mothers with small children, also sends a tape to new members as a gift. "I think it was through my sister-in-law who had older kids and also through a play group that I heard about *Veggie Tales* when my oldest son was three years old. He's now twelve. A woman at the play group kept going on and on about *Veggie Tales* and I wondered, what is this woman's deal!? At a play group someone would put on a show for the kids and it was often *Veggie Tales* at this woman's house."

Veggie Tales videos also figured prominently as advice from an older mother to a new mother. "A friend from church who already had kids when I had my first and said, 'You've got to get *Veggie Tales* videos.' We then started to get them from our church library, until grandma got a bunch of them for the kids."

Several mothers reported that they began watching the videos before they had kids because they became fans in high school or college, or their own youth group leaders would have kids who had the tapes. One mother reported that she and her husband would only get to see the videos rarely because they didn't have kids but would buy them for friends with kids, "so we started buying them for ourselves before kids. One time we got 'Rack, Shack and Benny' and when some friends were getting together and none of us had kids and we watched the video and had a great time."

Silly and Short

The fact that mothers could watch the tapes without gritted teeth speaks to the multilevel nature of the story lines and the number of popular culture jokes, such as a send-up of *Gilligan's Island*, that don't resonate with the preschool set but do with the mothers. Of course, the mothers didn't just have *Veggie Tales* for their kids; most also reported that their kids had *Thomas the Tank Engine* and, among the evangelical mothers, *Adventures in Odyssey* programs from Focus on the Family. *Veggies Tales* was notable, though, in its ability to generate enthusiasm.

Nearly all of the mothers reported that they encouraged their kids to view the series. Instead of telling kids to turn off the set and find other things to do, the mothers set aside special time in which their kids could watch the tapes. "I fell in love with them! I bought too many of them! Every day my children were allowed to watch 45 minutes of TV. I would always choose a tape over television because they had good moral teachings in it and they loved them. I think I went out and probably bought all of them."

Another mother said, "If we have a chunk of time, they are going to pop in a *Veggie Tale*. . . . I reach for a *Veggie Tale* because they are safe and they're short."

It was also important to the mothers that the series had something in it for them—it couldn't just be for the kids, as in the *Veggie Tales* version of the destruction of Jericho in which Joshua (played by Larry the Cucumber) leads the Israelites (played by the larger *Veggie Tales* cast) in marching around the walls of Jericho to "When the Saints Go Marching In," while the French Pea wall guards shoot grape slushy at the Israelites.

> I thought they were silly. At first I thought this isn't Biblically accurate, throwing slushies from the wall?! But as I sat back and thought, they have to make this so children can understand it. Children can probably understand being pelted by slushies, and being sticky. So I thought, O.K. But when we received the next one I thought they were fantastic. I actually have ones that are my favorites that I like to watch. My favorite is "King George and the Ducky." I love the music. I love the songs. It's hilarious. And I love "Larry Boy and the Big Fib" because it's funny how he introduces Larry to the whole thing. I love Larry, he's my favorite. It's because they have adult humor in there and I don't think the kids will get it. But the adults get the bigger picture of what they are talking about.

The role of the "bigger picture," as this mother put it, was important in the choice to get the *Veggie Tales* tapes, but not all agreed about what the larger goal of the series should be. Echoing the line given by Big Idea about Saturday morning fun and Sunday morning values, most fans agreed that the values in the series were as important as the catchy music and that those values were what made them choose the series over other popular kids' media. "That's an issue I have with Harry Potter, he cheats and he gets away with it. He gets away with breaking the rules. It turns what is wrong into good. They don't do that in *Veggie Tales*, if they break the rules, they get into trouble, and I like that."

Another fan compared the series to Disney in that the two brands offer similar production values, but "the Disney ones don't have a message or a negative one for the most part. It's fun to talk to the kids about the differences between the real Bible story and the *Veggie Tales* one, and how they just redid the Bible story in a fun way to communicate the message. The songs are a key part. I think the kids love the music and that's what we hear them singing all the time."

Again, as a departure from earlier claims that parents tried to shield their children from the media and worked to get their kids to reject media messages, these mothers actually encouraged viewing. "I love the *Veggie Tales* videos and encourage the kids to sit down and watch them . . . what better way to teach a child than by entertaining him or her."

Safe and Clean

A key word that surfaced in conversations with the mothers about media was *safe*. *Safe* seemed to describe media choices that didn't require monitoring, explanation, or censorship, and not only was the media devoid of violent or sexual images, it was also supportive of the families' moral beliefs. The words *safe*, *clean*, and *trust* came up over and over in nearly every interview. *Veggie Tales* scored high with mothers on the informal safe scale, which is probably why it was popular across both the evangelical and the more liberal households. *Safe* is also a term frequently used by Big Idea as a way to describe its offerings.

Some mothers described *safe* as meaning that they could pass on the tapes to others without fear of offending. "I think the kids watch that and then you know that they've seen a lot of others at the church and you know those are really safe to pass on, too. You know it doesn't have anything, you know, that other people with kids might not like. So I think that's good, too."

Safe is also a catchall term for media that's OK or not problematic.

> I would think that as far as the videotapes, safe on content. You don't have to worry so much.

> They [my children] are able to bring back truths that they've learned from the *Veggie Tales*. I also like the message in "The Toy That Saved Christmas" and "Rack, Shack and Benny." They all have a safe message.

> The kids can safely watch any of the shows; without me watching with them.

> The kids need to have safe materials. . . . The *Veggie Tales* presents good role models of how to act, like how kids speak to their parents.

Mothers frequently used a comparison with other media as a way of demonstrating what they liked about the series and why they chose it over other programs.

> If a cartoon is on that I don't like I reach for a *Veggie Tale* because they are safe and they're short.

> *Veggie Tale* tapes are pretty much safe, upbeat. I don't have to come in and fast-forward scary parts like in some other movies, and I can leave her alone with them and she catches on to them and learns pretty well from them, too.

Disney doesn't compare with *Veggie Tales* morally. *Veggie Tales* are way above in this area. They are comparable in all the other areas. They are great. They have a clear, concise story that I can trust! They have the same values we have and I'm never concerned about putting on a *Veggie Tale*.

Two mothers compared the series as similar in quality to Disney—an accolade that the *Veggie Tales* creators would surely relish—but

What I like about *Veggie Tales* that's better is I don't have to be as careful with *Veggie Tales*. With Disney I have to be careful with what the kids watch. My kids are not old enough to see Disney [her boys are 9 and 6] and I've previewed a lot of the films. The older Disney is scary and I don't want to introduce those kind of fears to the kids at this age. I don't have to worry about the content of the *Veggie Tales*.

It's much, much safer; to be fair Disney is certainly entertaining . . . but Disney often sends a message that is negative. I have to be discerning and follow up on shows. I use videos like a babysitter. . . . I put on a video and I don't have time or don't want to take the time to preview the videos, and I want something that is safe and I can go and get any *Veggie Tale* and put it on.

I think new Disney movies have blurred the lines between the good and the evil. The main characters are not admirable in all respects. The message from the older Disney movies is good, you have a clearly evil and a clearly good [character] throughout the movie. In *Veggie Tales* you are taking a story of thankfulness or like "Madame Blueberry" and the character that is not to be emulated is clear and Bob and Larry talk about it all through the movie. . . . The good and evil is easily discerned by the kids.

Although mothers were enthusiastic about the series, encouraged their children to watch the videos, and were avid purchasers of *Veggie Tales* merchandise like T-shirts, they, like the college students, had differing perceptions of the role of the series within the Christian media.

Safe Versus Saved

While more liberal mothers thought that the series was great be-cause "it doesn't impose itself" and the Bible is "not drummed into you," others made the distinction between *Veggie Tales* and media with a true Christian message—meaning a salvation-oriented message. The decision on the part of Big Idea to avoid mention of Jesus or salvation in favor of basic moral tales and Bible stories paid off by earning it a larger audience, but some more conservative evangelicals (both mothers and students) were disappointed with that choice.

Big Idea's own corporate statements avoided language that dealt with salvation or with espousing an entirely Christian point of view. The company claimed to embrace a Judeo-Christian worldview—a far cry from the sort of clear evangelical message learned by Phil Vischer in Bible college or the message desired by the more evangelical fans. It is clear, though, that the fans understood the dichotomy that Big Idea attempted to draw between the desire to be a value-oriented company and a com-pany with an evangelistic mission.

Some families, the more conservative ones, also encouraged their children to listen to *Adventures in Odyssey* tapes or read the Left Behind series or homeschool readers. Most fans agreed that the series was less likely to be problematic for the unchurched (but also less likely to be effectively evangelical) because of its focus on the Old Testament; some cited Jewish acquaintances who had the series or attempts to get Jewish friends to view the tapes. Some used the "soft-core" nature of the series to try to get other friends to view the tapes—for both evangelical and nonevangelical reasons.

> I'd definitely recommend them to people, my neighbors. I'd recommend them readily to church friends and unchurched friends, but I'd be careful to know the situation first.

> Some people don't like *Veggie Tales* because it's not right on the money biblically, but first you have to start them with the basics and this makes the basics real and at a kid's level. Some

people think they compromise to keep the kids' attention but I don't think they do. . . . It's a tool. It's not perfect but it's good and positive.

Some liberal mothers liked the series precisely because it wasn't salvation oriented.

You know, there are a lot of good people who are good but are not Christian and these are good foundation teachings, that, I think, everyone needs whether you're an adult or a child. Like, "Josh and the Big Wall," that would be good for Jewish people, too.

They probably are less offensive because they are Old Testament.

But many echoed critiques of Big Idea and *Veggie Tales* that were reminiscent of earlier critiques made about evangelical preachers Finney and Moody—not enough fire and brimstone, not enough specifics about salvation.

It bums me out that they don't give a stronger biblical message, the concrete stuff. It's not challenging enough or offensive enough. They share just the nice, nice stuff and that's good, but they have a great platform to share more, I wish sometimes they would share the salvation message. I would not buy this to give to a non-churched family as an outreach tool. It's a cute little video but it won't challenge their theology. But if that's not the goal for the *Veggie Tales* company that's OK. I wish they did more.

Other parents were concerned that their kids would be confused between *Veggie Tales* and Bible stories; that they'd miss the meaning of the falling walls of Jericho for all the flying slushy or the meaning of David and Goliath because David's sheep kept falling over.

I had to realize that you couldn't use it to teach a Bible story because they had changed it so much. I wanted to make sure that my kids know that sheep falling over was not in the Bible with David. So I wanted to make sure that they knew the difference between what the Bible story was and what the *Veggie Tale* story was. But, the big idea was there. So, as long as I wasn't using it to teach a Bible story with the *Veggie Tales* videos, I'm OK. So, I tend to like the ones that aren't based on a Bible story, like the ones that take the Big Lie or the Big Fib and I don't want the kids watching the Bible story ones as much, so they'd forget the Bible story.

But others found that the revisions of the stories helped their children learn the lessons and even helped one mother learn the story herself. "Actually, they were great at teaching Bible stories. Not being brought up with a Christian background I learned a lot of Bible stories I didn't know. Actually, when I think of 'Josh and the Big Wall' I still see the peas throwing ice cream cones or slushies. Most of my images of Bible stories are formed from *Veggie Tales* even though I read my Bible regularly."

One mother thought that the depictions produced by *Veggie Tales* of the stories might even be more accurate because of the opportunity for expansion. "It's not the whole Bible obviously, but I think that *Veggie Tales* seems a little more, or at least a few of them are a little more accurate when they are actually depicting a record from the Bible . . . because the stories are only a paragraph long."

Some mothers really seemed to wrestle with the role of pop culture Christianity and could see how *Veggie Tales* could be helpful in that it could draw people in, but they weren't willing to let it off the hook entirely or to let it be the sole source of religious media in the home. "I can use the *Veggie Tales* to assist in what we are already doing at home. The *Veggie Tales* can't stand on alone. It's not going to raise a Christian kid but we can certainly use them to go hand in hand with what [my husband] and I are already doing with the kids."

One mother said that she would use them as a means of educating her own children and leading them to adopt her religious beliefs. "My kids aren't saved, but they know who the Lord is and I will specifically choose programs that are Christian to watch. They enjoy the shows. . . . It's our lifestyle. They talk about the Lord; they connect with the message in them. My son preaches and plays church so it's our life."

Just as some mothers were a bit ambivalent about how *Veggie Tales* could fit into a committed evangelical Christian's life as anything but safe entertainment, the college students we spoke with were also concerned and, in some cases, harshly critical. One student said that it was easier to tell cute stories than it was to teach kids about principles such as sacrifice or sin. The students, again like some of the mothers, saw their religious beliefs best described as a relationship with God and were concerned that the series didn't "communicate a relational aspect with God, as opposed to just telling a story."

"My only concerns is that if it's, if they are all focusing on morals and everything, that it's just kinda reinforcing the idea that society has that Christianity is about set rules and if they could incorporate more of the relational aspect, you know, it will open onto the idea that it's more than set rules, it's about a relationship with God."

One student said that God is represented in the series as a kind of Superdad with household rules to follow, but another student said that the series doesn't address the parenting commands of the Bible. "We communicate to kids to fear your parents because they spank you. We believe that's a biblical mandate. It think it would be really good for Christianity to deal, like start teaching kids a broader, like not just teach kids about the aspects of God that are easy to adore him, but also the aspects of God that are hard to, hard to enjoy sometimes."

One obvious distinction between the students' opinion of the series and that of the mothers is that the mothers are charged with parenting, while the students are simply evaluating the series from a more adult standpoint. It is interesting, though, that the students are arguing for a "tougher" Christianity and God and that they want the series to be more challenging. In fact, they wanted all of Christian media to be more challenging. They also were critical of media for reasons that are often mentioned in the scholarly and medical literature, but weren't mentioned by the mothers; they were critical of the time that is lost to television. "When you are sitting and watching TV for an hour and a half a day . . . then you don't read your Bible and you say that you don't have time."

Another student said that the Christian media is just there to be a replacement distraction, not to actually turn one's mind and heart to God. "Though I only listen to Christian music, like I was really using the Christian music to turn my thoughts toward God, it was just there to keep me occupied, you know, so like even Christian media, perhaps even like Christian fiction just can be a detractor rather instead of actually spurring us on."

The students seemed to want Christian media to be less about entertainment and less about holding an audience and more about confronting fans. This is ironic because the industry, within its new corporate framework, needs to garner audiences in order to stay alive. One student said that without that kind of challenge, people will begin to follow God only to become disillusioned. "It causes them to not be great followers of God, because when God is not that Fudgesicle they envisioned him to be, they ditch it, they drop it."

The students said that they expected Christian companies to have a clearer vision of evangelism rather than marketing—they didn't mention economic realities as a potential challenge but saw that the course taken by the Christian media certainly had the potential to be more profitable. "Is the purpose outreach? Is the purpose to draw Christians? Groups need to draw a clear line in the sand. *Veggie Tales* needs to draw a clear line in the sand, saying like 'here's our purpose.'"

The trends criticized in the Christian media were also noted as existing in churches. The students said that the Christian churches they had attended had relied too much on trendy music and fancy graphics and gimmicks and too little on a challenging and persuasive message and believing that the message itself should be enough.

When Christian churches start appealing to our [attention spans], it's buying into the fact that they have got to keep changing themselves of getting new trendy things to keep our attention, where as it should be the reverse where us Christians should be taking an active discipline to keep ourselves focused on Christianity in itself and when they are changing like that all the time, they're communicating a message that what we are about is not good enough in itself for you to desire and want it. We have to change it to make it appeal to you to attract you to it. It's like, what we believe in is not attractive in itself.

Some students said that *Veggie Tales*, and other Christian media, was putting people in danger by making non-Christians believe that they are OK with God, when they are not, according to conservative Protestant theology. In other words, *Veggie Tales* could be putting viewers in danger of believing that they won't go to hell if they behave properly instead of saying, as one student put it, "You're incomplete. You need a relationship with Jesus."

Many of the students, though, saw the point of making the Bible relevant as a way of leading people to salvation, but only if the message itself doesn't get changed. "I think a lot of churches, you get so caught up in relevance and all people want to be somewhere that's happy, people don't want to hear about the sins, people want to know they're loved and they won't think they're loved if we bring up something that makes you uncomfortable so we end up changing parts of the message that make them uncomfortable."

One student was particularly cognizant of the history of Protestantism, and when I questioned him about the historical role of printed materials in proselytizing he said, "People used to show their faith personally and they had a Bible, but if they didn't that's word of mouth and initiating conversations." At that point another student jumped in: "So we have become dependent on the media to do the sharing rather than ourselves which I think is another huge problem."

The students seemed to really relate to the difficulty in making a personal connection for the purpose of evangelism. They talked as a group about the difficulty in attempting to share their faith with others. This gave them a certain, very concrete insight into how making some Christian media more accessible is similar to their own discomfort with confronting others. "I mean . . . I knock on someone's door and I say 'I'm just here to do a survey with you' when my intentions really are that we can have a conversation, relate, have interests so it could be strategic in a way. . . . I mean, I don't think I'm deceiving someone when I come to their door but there is an aspect of like I want to relate to them. It's like I need to think that at least gives them a chance to say, yes, I'm willing to talk to you." Another student continued, saying, "Yeah, it's if you open the door and say 'Hi I'm here to share Jesus with you.'" And then another student provided the key analysis: "I'm here to tell you how you are a sinner, do you have a minute?"

With this connection to their own personal experiences of evangelism, the students seemed to reach the ambivalence present in a lot of Christian media that they spoke about. Their concerns were different from those of the mothers, who seemed predominantly concerned with their children's safety in a media-saturated world; the students were concerned with trying to live up to the mandate that Christianity seemed to present to them without being ostracized by their friends.

So in some ways, the students came back around to supporting the goals of Christian media as a way of finding an "opportunity to share the Gospel," but they also were still critical of Christian media, particularly musicians who had "crossed over." I mentioned the rise of Amy Grant and her ability to find audiences in both the Christian and mainstream markets, but they really didn't resonate with Grant—instead they mentioned Stacie Orrico as the artist who embodied that imperfect balance between evangelism and acceptance seeking they were concerned about.

> She [Stacie Orrico] had a whole CD like it was all Christian but she came out with a new CD, and it was on a Christian label and all of the songs were just about God, but she does have one about waiting by the phone for this guy to call her. . . . But when this song was released to the secular radio stations, then other people like Stacie Orrico now. . . . She actually said that she did the song because she wanted to be able to relate to all audiences and said that it was a good way to get all audiences to buy the CD.

The students then came back to the experience of doing face-to-face evangelism and how hard it is for them, and that gave them some connection with Orrico's (and *Veggie Tales*') walking the fine line between a challenging message and an entertaining one. "Yeah, that scares the life out of you, but who do we really revere, who do we really trust? We face a lot less than the apostles did but they didn't fear whole crowds." But then another student said, "But I'm seeking an opportunity to share the Gospel. This [the music and cartoons] is a way to survive an opportunity because . . . people just don't respond to strangers well . . . and everyone's plugged into their MP3 player."

The student's statement about the MP3 player reminds me of just how diverse the media choices are for all segments of society. It's not just the book or the movie. It's also the game, the lunchbox, the magazine, the compact disc. Consumers expect to express themselves via mass retail products that touch every aspect of their lives. A bumper sticker isn't enough. You also need the right theme for your date book and the right cover for your cell phone.

References

Baranick, A. (1997, October 18). Eating up Veggie Tales; Kids, adults love Christian videos. *The Plain Dealer* (Cleveland), p. 4E.

Bendroth, M. L. (1996). Fundamentalism and the media, 1930–1990. In D. A. Stout and J. M. Buddenbaum (Eds.), *Religion and mass media: Audiences and adaptations*, 74–84. Thousand Oaks, CA: Sage.

Buddenbaum, J. M. (1996). Use of mass media for political information in a Middletown Quaker meeting. In D. A. Stout and J. M. Buddenbaum (Eds.), *Religion and mass media: Audiences and adaptations*, 197–210. Thousand Oaks, CA: Sage.

Buddenbaum, J. M., & Hoover, S. M. (1996). The role of religion in public attitudes toward religion news. In D. A. Stout and J. M. Buddenbaum (Eds.), *Religion and mass media: Audiences and adaptations*. Thousand Oaks, CA: Sage.

Campus Life. (1998 September–October). Tales from the crisper! p. 54.

Carey, J. (1997). The communications revolution and the professional communicator. In E. S. Munson and C. A. Warren (Eds.), *James Carey: A Critical Reader*, 128–143. Minneapolis: University of Minnesota Press.

Clark, L. S. (2003). *From angels to aliens: Teenagers, the media and the supernatural*. New York: Oxford.

Hamilton, N. F., & Rubin, A. M. (1992). The influence of religiosity on television viewing. *Journalism Quarterly* 69(3), 667–678.

Hoover, S. M. (1990). The religious television audience: A matter of significance or size? In R. Abelman and S. Hoover (Eds.), *Religious television: Controversies and conclusions*, 109–130. Norwood, NJ: Ablex.

Hoover, S. M., Clark, L. S., & Alters, D. F. (2004). *Media, home and family*. New York: Routledge.

Hoover, S. M., & Venturelli, S. (1996). The category of the religious: The blindspot of contemporary media theory? *Critical Studies in Mass Communication*, 13 (September), 251–265.

Jelen, T. (1996). Catholicism, conscience, and censorship. In D. A. Stout and J. M. Buddenbaum (Eds.), *Religion and mass media: Audiences and adaptations*. Thousand Oaks, CA: Sage.

Krendl, K., & Clark, G. (1993). Preschoolers and VCRs in the home: A multiple methods approach. *Journal of Broadcasting and Electronic Media* 37(3), 20.

Linderman, A. (1997). Making sense of religion in television. In S. Hoover and K. Lundby (Eds.), *Rethinking media, religion, and culture*, 263–282. Thousand Oaks, CA: Sage.

Lindlof, T. (1996). The passionate audience: Community inscriptions of *The Last Temptation of Christ*. In D. A. Stout and J. M. Buddenbaum (Eds.), *Religion and mass media: Audiences and adaptations*, 148–168. Thousand Oaks, CA: Sage.

McDannell, C. (1995). *Material christianity: Religion and popular culture in America*. New Haven, CT: Yale University Press.

McFarland, S. G., & Warren, J. C. (1992). Religious orientations and selective exposure among fundamentalist Christians. *Journal for the Scientific Study of Religion* 31(2), 163–174.

Morgan, M. (1973). *The total woman*. Old Tappan, NJ: Spire.

Radway, J. (1991). *Reading the romance*. Chapel Hill: University of North Carolina Press.

Rimmer, T. (1996). Religion, mass media, and tolerance for civil liberties. In D. A. Stout and J. M. Buddenbaum (Eds.), *Religion and mass media: Audiences and adaptations*, 105–122. Thousand Oaks, CA: Sage.

Roof, C. (1997). Blurred boundaries: Religion and prime time television. In M. Suman (Ed.), *Religion and prime time television*, 61–68. Westport, CT: Praeger.

Scott, D. W. (2003). Mormon "family values" versus television: An analysis of the discourse of Mormon couples regarding television and popular media culture. *Critical Studies in Mass Communication* 20(3), 317–333.

Shrewsbury, A. (1998). A tale of two veggies: Disney meets Monty Python meets the Bible in a Christian video series for children that has exploded in popularity—among adults. *The Omaha World Herald*, p. 1.

Stout, D. A. (1996). Protecting the family: Mormon teachings about mass media. In D. A. Stout and J. M. Buddenbaum (Eds.), *Religion and mass media: Audiences and adaptations*, 85–100. Thousand Oaks, CA: Sage.

Valenti, J. M., & Stout, D. A. (1996). Diversity from within: An analysis of the impact of religious culture on media use and effective communication to women. In D. A. Stout and J. M. Buddenbaum (Eds.), *Religion and mass media: Audiences and adaptations*, 183–196. Thousand Oaks, CA: Sage.

Warren, H. (1998). Standing against the tide: Conservative Protestant families, mainstream and Christian media. Dissertation, University of Texas.

Wuthnow, R. (1988). *The restructuring of American Religion*. Princeton, NJ: Princeton University Press.

6

Looking for Values in All Sorts of Places

How to use VeggieBucks: VeggieBucks are a way for you to help introduce children to VeggieTales videos! Children may use a VeggieBucks coupon to get $2.00 off the purchase of a VeggieTales video.

—from the VeggieTown Values for the Family! Vacation Bible School program

Some really fun stuff . . . Dress-up Mix-up Larry, Bounce 'n Talk Veggies, Sing 'n Dance Bob & Larry, Junior Asparagus Bedtime Friend . . . by Fisher-Price

—from a promotional insert in a *Veggie Tales* video

VeggieTales Fabric Quilting Squares, Nativity Set, Cake Pan, Bible Cover, Bob and Larry Growth Chart, Kids Dishes, Chick-fil-A key rings

—from eBay

As Phil Vischer said about the relationship between other kids' media and the toys that are marketed along with them—it doesn't matter what the message of the video is if the only toys to play with celebrate antisocial messages. Big Idea created the sort of all-encompassing media and peripheral product universe that would keep kids and families in their own Veggie land. From the products described above to party plates and cups and from video games to cross promotions with Ministry to Mothers of Preschoolers, Auntie Anne's pretzels, Langers juice, Sea-World, and Chuck E. Cheese's, Big Idea learned to license its products to extend its brand.

What Does Mass Retail Need With a Christian Video Series?

As demonstrated by the growth of the *Veggie Tales* brand when it was stocked by the mass retailers Wal-Mart and Target, leaving the Christian bookstore niche was necessary for the development of the series and its audience. However, Big Idea is not the only beneficiary of the arrangement. Mass retailers have learned that the Christian market is large and profitable. The biggest retailer of Christian items is Wal-Mart (*Forbes*, 2004), and it's safe to say that Wal-Mart doesn't carry these products out of a sense of Christian charity. In fact, until Mel Gibson's *The Passion of the Christ* drowned it out, *Jonah—A Veggie Tales Movie* was the highest-grossing Christian-themed movie of recent times, according to *Forbes*. Of course, not every viewer of *The Passion* was an evangelical Christian and not every purchaser of *The Purpose-Driven Life* is, either, but these products tend to appeal to the kind of consumer targeted by Wal-Mart and Sears and Target: family-oriented with disposable income but still looking for value (and values). In fact, *Veggie Tales* is identified as the number one brand to follow by both Christian media producers and retail product investors, according to Michael Pachter, an analyst with Wedbush Morgan Securities (*Forbes*, 2004).

The success of Christian merchandise in the mainstream retail environment was initially limited to music by artists such as Amy Grant—artists whose music had a message ambiguous enough to be interpreted as not about religion. While that's still true and that ambiguity about Christianity has served *Veggie Tales* well, even more overtly Christian products are doing well in stores. This most likely indicates that retailers have discovered that Christians have been in their stores all along. As Kmart's spokesman Dennis Wigent said, "the reason we're putting these products in our stores is because our customers want them. The market continues to increase and we have to keep expanding to keep up with the demand" (Hogan-Albach, 1998). Another children's video series, *Tails from the Ark*, avoids using direct Bible verses in its stories because the creator hoped that "Tails would appeal more broadly to families of other faiths besides Christianity" (Ashdown, 2001). Further, some see the Christian market as a path into the mainstream. "Though he's hesitant to say so, Davis [the director of sales and marketing for the production studio] acknowledges that using the Christian retail channel to launch a new family series is often an effective way of gaining access to the general retail market, and it's a strategy that he hopes will work for Tails" (Ashdown, 2001).

Lower Production Costs, Rising Market Entries

One reason why it's been easier for Christian media producers to break into all aspects of the mainstream retail and media industry is the falling cost of production involving computer technologies. As the technologies have become less expensive and more user-friendly, it has become easier for smaller shops to create high-quality products for consumers accustomed to Disney quality. One aspect of the success of Big Idea is tied to Phil Vischer and Mike Nawrocki's early knowledge of key computer-generated animation software and equipment and their savvy in knowing their animation limits. It was a wise choice to limit the depiction of vegetables to what they could produce quickly and professionally rather than to risk an amateurish product. Consumers who are fans of *Toy Story* and Nickelodeon are unlikely to be patient with cut-rate animation even if it has a message they want. Similarly, the early success of Focus on the Family in the Christian entertainment market was tied to radio—a medium that is unique for its ability to sound far more expensive than it is, and the means of broadcasting and recording have not advanced in a dramatic or expensive fashion. (Of course, this doesn't include a move to satellite radio, or the federal mandates involving digital television, but the costs associated with producing tapes, analog broadcasts, and even CDs have not grown dramatically.)

In addition, series such as *Bibleman* and others released by Tommy Nelson and Dr. Laura Schlessinger have found that both using the series to create licensed product opportunities and using existing publicity (in Dr. Laura's case) help boost media that doesn't have the advantage of broadcast and cable exposure. Tommy Nelson's marketing representatives told *Kidscreen*, an industry publication, that they feel it's their mission to reach all Christians wherever they are with the company's message (Ashdown, 2001).

Break on Through to the Other Side

Beyond the video industry, and ironic given the competition and distrust voiced by some Christian media producers, some Christian music artists have found an outlet with Radio Disney, according to the Gospel Music Association (GMA). This is a realistic reaction to the decreasing role of Christian retailers and another means of reaching the audience that spends more of its time in Target or Wal-Mart than other outlets. Frank Breeden, the president of the Gospel Music Association, welcomes the shift in retailers because although sales in Christian retailers have been down in recent years, overall sales have been up, and that discrepancy can be attributed to the mass retailers' stocking Christian artists. "Perhaps more than ever, mainstream retailers and marketers are recognizing that the Christian music buyer is an attractive target for the goods and services they offer, beyond the sales of music. Additionally, we've seen an increase in the number of major companies establishing relationships with Christian artists, providing even greater visibility for Christian music beyond the Christian retail market" (GMA Media Relations, 2002).

Of course, the use of the Christian bookseller as a springboard, but not as the exclusive source of certain media, has created problems in the Christian retail industry. Retailers have seen the brands they took a chance on and promoted thrive, but they haven't been a part of the success. Fewer booksellers are attending the CBA (formerly the Christian Booksellers Association) annual convention, and topics at the convention have included how Christian retailers can reinvent themselves to become less dispensable—at least to their customers. Even stalwart publishers such as Thomas Nelson have cut back on booth space and presence at the convention as the Christian retail market has suffered a 5 percent loss in market share (Garrett, Riess, & Tickle, 2003).

Aside from the dominance of big box stores in many areas of retailing besides Christian merchandise, another reason for the growth of the overall Christian media segment during a decline in market share for Christian retail has to do with how Christian products are developed and marketed. Like *Veggie Tales*, constructed to appeal to a broader audience, and the other video titles mentioned above, publishers like Nelson and Zondervan have pushed to broaden the market for religious titles. Piggybacking on the renewed interest in religion and spirituality, as well as the boom in self-help titles and gurus, Christian publishers have found that they can continue to appeal to their traditional base while pushing the margins further. Books such as *The Purpose-Driven Life* effectively reach both audiences, and author tours frequently include stops at both Christian and mainstream retailers. Of course some Christian booksellers refuse to stock titles that may be seen as New Age, but that simply pushes more of those titles (and customers) into finding new places to sell (and shop for) books.

Just What Is the Christian Media Industry and Who Is Its Audience?

This flexibility in the market and the desire of publishers to appeal to a number of different audiences with the same text has created problems in assessing the size and strength of the industry (Nelson, 2003). Is *The Purpose-Driven Life* a Christian title? Does a product have to include a call to salvation in order to qualify as Christian? Does it have to mention Jesus? Or God? Can "personal growth" appropriately be considered a home for Christian literature, and if Dr. Phil, Jack Canfield, and Dr. James Dobson share the same section, can those sales be effectively categorized as Christian? And beyond marketing campaigns and shelf labels, does the affiliation of the publisher automatically qualify or disqualify certain products? Zondervan, owned by HarperCollins, a subsidiary of News Corporation, doesn't look like a Christian publisher if one examines its organizational chart, but it publishes some of the biggest names in Christian publishing. Zondervan's sales, though, are split pretty evenly between Christian and mainstream retailers (Leith, 2001). Similarly, if a book or video captures an audience beyond the conservative Protestant market, such as is the case with the Left Behind series, does the diversity of the audience change the characterization of the book? One thing is clear, though: the audience for these books is attractive regardless of the retailer. This audience buys books (Nelson, 2003) and buys them in hardcover.

Christian Retail Plays the Mainstream Market Game

But Christian retailers aren't giving up easily, and as the overall market segment has grown, so have some retailers. The market is coming to be dominated by chains such as Moments with Majesty and Lifeway, who can purchase on volume and offer competitive discounts, and, as in many other industries, mom-and-pop retailers are closing and making way for the chains. In addition, the segment will probably maintain a viable niche status as a place where evangelicals can find a level of depth and breadth in the genre that wouldn't make economic sense for mainstream retailers. As Kelly Gallagher, the vice president for marketing and technology for the Evangelical Christian Publishers Association, writes in his assessment of the industry,

Christian retail stands at the crossroad. While it is true that market erosion has occurred in the past several years due to the growing popularity of Christian products in the mainstream marketplace, it is also true that it still maintains the dominant role in being the single largest channel to sell Christian-based books, music, gifts, and other product. Commitment to increasing the efficiency of the supply chain will play a critical role in determining whether or not that position can be maintained in the years to come. (Gallagher, 2003)

In the area of marketing to kids, Christian retailers are loath to cede ground to big boxes. Instead, they are vowing to woo kids with the kinds of choices that they can't get elsewhere, and publishers' willingness to repackage content in multiple ways is seen as a boon to retailers who want to provide a sort of mainstream selection within the Christian retail environment. The post-9/11 environment is seen as pushing the audience to stay home and reconnect with their families and their churches, and the industry sees this as an opportunity. The *CBA Marketplace* on-line newsletter offers point-by-point alternatives to mainstream choices that will help its members demonstrate that they do have what their core audience is looking for. Kids seeking Harry Potter? Offer the C. S. Lewis "Narnia" titles. The interest in reality television among teens is met with a reality mission series documenting "twentysomethings on a 40,000-mile, Gospel-preaching journey—complete with lions and leeches" (CBA, 2003). The CBA also encourages its members to both hop on the "brainy baby" bandwagon and actively seek the Spanish-speaking market. The Christian retail segment is determined to no longer be a once-a-year stop for a confirmation Bible or a gift plaque; it wants to be as hip as a Vineyard worship service.

Changing Retail Environment, Changing Message

Through the willingness of both publishers and retailers to broaden the market, the message of much Christian media has changed from sermonizing and salvation to a more soothing message. "Today Christian living titles offer more of a gentle message on how you need to apply your life. They're more anecdotal, more compassionate, and they're reaching a broader audience, which is good. They've made Christianity more approachable," Greg Petree, the vice president of marketing for Howard Publishing, told *Publishers Weekly* (Kiesling, 2004).

Of course, the willingness of the industry to reach its audience while embracing popular culture trends isn't new, although the diversity and size of publishers certainly is. In addition, as Colleen McDannell documents in *Material Christianity*, debates over how far one should go to sell T-shirts and exercise videos aren't new either (McDannell, 1995). McDannell points out that the industry originated in the late nineteenth century, when domestic piety encouraged religious objects in the home. Once these materials gained a foothold in the home, the market exploded in two ways. First, changes in manufacturing technology and transportation allowed for the mass creation of goods and the ability to distribute them. Second, advertising encouraging purchasing and the willingness of Christians to publicize their beliefs meant that the market could continue to grow beyond a cross on the wall and a family Bible. Capitalizing on this interest in home furnishings and other faith-related materials, the Gospel Trumpet Company was founded in the late nineteenth century to manufacture and sell products and to serve the self-assigned mission of its owner to "reinforce authentic Christian truth" (McDannell, 1995, 231). The company operated hand in hand with the Church of God, according to McDannell, and developed an extensive line of merchandise from note cards to placemats, pencils, and lamps, which were sold not just as note cards, placemats, pencils, and lamps, but as Christian note cards, Christian placemats, Christian pencils, and Christian lamps. Some manufactured images of Jesus were so widely distributed that they, in many ways, have come to dominate the popular imagination of what Jesus physically looked like. But again, the mission of the company appears to have been more to save souls than make money.

McDannell also documents class splits in using religious materials in home decoration and notes that Catholics and working-class Protestants were unwilling to trade their paintings and mottoes for the streamlined, modern aesthetic (McDannell, 1995). The growth of the industry in post–World War II America allowed for marketing to a wide range of tastes with products from wall plaques for traditional families to "Jesus Christ: He's the real thing" patches that both echoed the ubiquitous Coca-Cola slogan and 1970s casual clothing. With each trend the Christian industry has reinvented itself to meet the desires of the audience shaped by popular culture, and this has meant Victorian wall plaques, T-shirts, "classy" Reagan-era jewelry, and media items that echo mainstream products with a Christian spin.

Manufacturers and marketers of Christian merchandise have responded to both developments in media and trends in popular taste, but until relatively recently, these products have remained in specialty stores, mail order outlets, and direct mail. Aside from the selection of Precious Moments figurines in Hallmark stores, one had to go looking for Christian merchandise. But now there's both an upswing in interest and sales and downward pressure on prices as the product segment enters the broader retail environment. In many ways, these changes in the market mirror some of the changes that helped televangelism thrive in the first half of the twentieth century.

Making Media That Sells and Saves

While some might see the movement of Christian merchandise as simply a sign of the times, a mark of success for the evangelical movement, or a terrifying notice for those who are concerned about a conservative Christian majority, one should take note of these changes because they are portents of not just how the retail environment has changed overall, but how those changes may affect what merchandise and what messages are available for consumers. The desire of the market to maximize profits and reach ever-larger markets efficiently will encourage retailers to stock products that offer something to everyone. Developers of more exclusively constructed merchandise intended to challenge the majority culture or to spur the evangelical to action may not find a home for their product on the shelves if it is seen as potentially offensive or, worse, a poor seller.

Just as conservative evangelicals learned how to use the restrictive broadcast environment to compete effectively on television, merchandisers have had to learn to work within the structure and pressures of the retail environment. In the case of *Veggie Tales*, in which most of Big Idea's exposure came in the bookstore environment, rather than on television, the success of the series and its related products depended heavily on the ability of the company to form the kinds of partnerships necessary for efficiently exploiting the market. Just as Dallas Smythe noted in his landmark work on political economy in broadcasting in the 1950s, the technologies have forced structure and centralization on the industry that have become necessary for success (Smythe, 1957).

The Role of Economic Structures in Shaping the Religious Message

The economics of merchandising and media shape children's video—even children's video produced for religious or evangelical ends. It is impossible for the producers of even the most benign, pro-social message to evade the realities of the marketplace (McChesney, 2000). As Peter Wilkin writes in *The Political Economy of Global Communication*, media markets are not open and free to those who lack the financial capacity to compete within them. It is necessary to make a profit in order to continue to invest in producing more media. Wilkin further writes that nonmajority perspectives will have a difficult time gaining traction in the culture unless these perspectives are able to gain currency so that they might challenge the mainstream conceptions. "Hence, the ownership and control of the means of communication is a vital issue for human autonomy and security precisely because it is the means of communication that lies at the heart of the possibility for meaningful political analysis, discussion and criticism or existing institutions and ways of doing things" (Wilkin, 2001).

Further, the relationship between economic structures and media production allows one to create "a more sophisticated understanding of how meaning is made and re-made through the concrete activities of producers and consumers" (Boyd-Barrett, 1995). Of course, this behavior on the part of media and markets isn't new, but this activity is accelerating in the realm of Christian media. Like most media, Christian media began as a small-scale program of production and direct sales, but the relationship between the producer and consumer was altered by the separation necessitated by distribution agreements and licensing arrangements. The need of the Christian media to gain a foothold in the mainstream retail market was matched by the need of the media conglomerate for diversification (Murdock & Golding, 1995). Major conglomerates didn't suddenly "get religion"; what they got was a need for diversification so that if hip-hop sales fall, gospel might remain stable. HarperCollins did with its ownership portfolio what many do with retirement accounts: purchase a variety of investments so as to minimize risk. This need for diversification, along with the Christian media producers' need for a large, market-savvy partner, allowed for the creation of critical partnerships that would not only put *The Prayer of Jabez* on the shelves at Wal-Mart, but also influence tastes to make it a top-selling brand.

The Role of Licensing in Shaping Media Messages

In the arena of children's toys and media, Ellen Seiter documents the role of the toy peripherals that go along with a media program in shaping the program itself. Licensing, the means by which the *Veggie Tales* series begets Junior Asparagus dolls and kiddie plates and bowls, has become more and more central in media programming. Seiter documents the role of licensing potential in determining whether some characters will even make it into programming (Seiter, 1995). She cites one trade journal as ranking upcoming children's television programs solely on the basis of the anticipated success of each program's licensing arrangements (Seiter, 1995).

Of course, while children do have an increasingly large role to play in the consumer market, products that appeal to kids as well as adults are still desirable. Particularly in the area of young children's videos and music, where the parent expects to spend hours on end listening to a given program, the need of the program to reach both audiences is paramount. This is underscored in the audience reactions to *Veggie Tales*, where mothers repeatedly spoke about their own enjoyment of the series, and college-aged young adults also talked about watching the series for their own enjoyment. *Veggie Tales* has ridden a trend apparent in more secular children's entertainment programs with this ability to appeal to multiple audiences. As Heather Hendershot writes about Nickelodeon, that channel "succeeds, in large part, by simultaneously satisfying children and adults" (Hendershot, 2004). Like Nickelodeon, *Veggie Tales* doesn't talk down to kids and doesn't use violence that would worry adults. In *Veggie Tales'* case the programs also have enough values, coupled with enough fun, that parents can have their children watch the series, buy the toys, and read the books with the knowledge that not only are they "safe," but they might even teach their kids about values, too. As with the breakfast cereal that is both tasty and nutritious, a mother would almost be remiss in not encouraging a devotion to *Veggie Tales*.

Marketers count on this kind of broad appeal within a niche that is easily targeted. Nickelodeon also proved, at about the same time that *Veggie Tales* was in its infancy, that there was a market for children's programming with interesting plots and appeal to kids, teens, and adults. When Nickelodeon added toy marketing to the mix as a second act, rather than the first act previously used by Care Bears and Smurfs, the combination was dramatic (Hendershot, 2004). Hendershot documents that not only did advertising across all children's television reach $1 billion annually, but there was additional interest in the young child market (Kapur, 1999; Hendershot, 2004). With *Veggie Tales*, Big Idea entered the market that Nickelodeon had recently demonstrated to be a winner, but it also tested its franchise in the laboratory of Christian bookstores and made a dramatic leap forward in terms of the quality of Christian kids' programming. Of course there would be interest not only from the Christian audience but also from the media retailer and conglomerate.

Veggie Tales and *Jay Jay the Jet Plane*

Let's look at two examples of the movement between the Christian media industry and the mainstream market: *Veggie Tales*, of course, and *Jay Jay the Jet Plane*. Elsewhere I've documented the growth of Big Idea and *Veggie Tales*, but *Jay Jay* has a quite different history, which also makes it notable. *Jay Jay* "follows the adventures of a perky and curious six-year-old jet plane . . . and his airplane friends" (Porchlight Entertainment, 2004). *Jay Jay* was created by David and Deborah Michel of WonderWings .com Entertainment "to provide wholesome, positive role models . . . through whimsical stories, a family of airplanes and the caring adult figure, Brenda Blue" (Wonderwings.com Entertainment, 2004). The creators' website goes on to thank God for the inspiration to create the series.

Jay Jay airs on PBS and is distributed to over sixty countries through arrangements with Porchlight Entertainment (Porchlight Entertainment, 2003a). Porchlight also distributes episodic and movie-length programming to PAX, NBC, and the Disney Channel, and while *Jay Jay* is not its only "values-oriented" distribution property, the company is diverse in its library. What's interesting about *Jay Jay*, beyond the fact that it was created by a values-oriented company but has achieved a wide audience, is that is has consciously created a dual market.

Beyond the agreements with PBS and other outlets both domestic and international, *Jay Jay* and Porchlight market distinctly different properties to the Christian and mainstream retail markets. Porchlight partners with Tommy Nelson, a division of the religious bookseller Thomas Nelson, to distribute *Inspirational Baby*, a new entry in the smart baby media category. *Inspirational Baby* was created, in part, through consultation with faculty of the Fuller Theological Seminary, according to Porchlight's press releases (Porchlight Entertainment, 2003b). Porchlight also produces *Adventures from the Book of Virtues*.

Porchlight's arrangement with Tommy Nelson gives it access to the dedicated Christian retail market along with a continued presence in the mainstream market. Tommy Nelson's website provides a clearinghouse of titles of interest to Christian families, from the *Adventures in Odyssey* series from Focus on the Family to Max Lucado and *The Prayer of Jabez*. Tommy Nelson offers *Jay Jay the Jet Plane* in "special episodes especially for Christian families" and touts the series as showing "toddlers Scriptural truths" (Tommy Nelson, 2004). *Jay Jay* is also an example of the role of Tommy Nelson in moving Christian material from a number of Christian producers to both the mainstream and the Christian markets; *Jay Jay*, the Christian version, is created in collaboration with Focus on the Family and sold through both Focus and Tommy Nelson.

This savvy working of both the Christian and mainstream retail markets presents one means by which Christian media producers can remain distinct from larger conglomerates. Alternatively, Zondervan, a formerly independent Christian publisher, who partnered frequently with Big Idea and *Veggie Tales*, is now part of HarperCollins and tends to present media that can cross markets rather than distinct media for each market. Zondervan has been a division of HarperCollins since 1988 (Zondervan, 2003), but it still maintains a distinctive presence as a Christian publisher. However, its independence within the conglomerate has been restrained by HarperCollins. HarperCollins, for example, has the contract to publish Narnia materials to accompany the anticipated Disney film, and Zondervan has been explicitly cut out of the plan to develop its own coordinated media. It also maintains the product group Zonderkidz, which is the book publishing home of *Veggie Tales*.

It is interesting to note, however, that despite the careful attention in Zondervan's press material to the publishing house's Christian roots, little mention of that is made in some of the pitches for *Veggie Tales* products. For example, the Zondervan website mentions that the corporate headquarters features Christian New Testament Bible verses and a sculpture depicting Jesus, but sales materials for *Veggie Tales* books tout sales figures and new releases, not God. Zondervan also lists strategic alliances with groups such as Promise Keepers and Focus on the Family, but sales materials for the *Jonah*-related products avoid mentioning God until the last sentence. This is consistent, however, with the positioning of Big Idea within the marketplace as a "family media company" that provides products reflecting a "Judeo-Christian worldview" (Zondervan, 2003).

Jay Jay and *Veggie Tales* represent two ways in which Christian media producers have successfully exploited the prevailing political economy of the current media environment. Overtly Christian messages are difficult to get shelved outside of Christian bookstores, but a "values-based" message is not only acceptable, but popular. In addition, larger firms looking to diversify are willing to work with Christian and religious products in the hopes of capturing an audience that might go elsewhere. One issue to consider, though, is whether the content is being shaped by the needs of the market and whether that shaping influences the religious experience and practice of consumers. If people go to the book sections of Wal-Mart, Target, and Barnes & Noble seeking in a manner that used to send people to church on Sundays, what are they finding? Media of all types are proliferating, but the universe within which messages diversify is rather narrow. If Wal-Mart sells Christianity, then how distinctive can that message be? One can talk about values, and "God loves you," but can a challenging series survive? What about a message that is somewhat exclusionary? Dr. James Dobson's Focus on the Family titles on parenting are prominent on the Wal-Mart website, but one must search through pages to find Ryan Dobson's *To Die For: The Dangerous Truth About Following Christ*, and one must search specifically to find *Marriage Under Fire: Why We Must Win This Battle*, Dr. James Dobson's argument for banning gay marriage.

Projecting to a Blank Screen

Returning to the topic of *Veggie Tales*, what fans of the series seem to be interested in are the characters and the image of the series as happy and safe. The eBay sales notices at the top of this chapter don't call the shoppers' attention to the Judeo-Christian message of the series that can be reinforced through the cute quilting squares; instead, the images on the quilting squares reinforce the happy image of the series. In this way, the happy but somewhat bland image of Bob and Larry reminds me of my son's attraction to Elmo: he loves Elmo but has no actual interest in anything Elmo says or does. Elmo appears to be the proxy for happiness, dancing and singing the "Elmo's World" song, not for learning. Elmo is a celebrity in my house because he's Elmo, and Bob and Larry are loved for being Bob and Larry, not because they tell Bible stories.

What this means is that the market is, in some ways, shaping the message. It might not matter if the message is the length of skirts or the color of cars, but if the message about faith is shaped according to what will sell online or in a mass retail outlet, does that ultimately shape some of the direction of faith in the culture? To be sure, messages of faith have always been shaped by what's acceptable in a given culture, but what's new is the degree to which this shaping is done by the economic rationality of the market.

References

Ashdown, S. (2001, July 1). Christian kidvid converts more consumers. *Kidscreen.*

Boyd-Barrett, O. (1995). The political economy approach. In O. Boyd-Barrett and C. Newbold (Eds.), *Approaches to media: A reader*, 186–192. London: Arnold.

CBA. (2003). *Are you listening? What kids want now.* Retrieved October 22, 2003, from www.cbaonline.org/MarketPlace/kidstrends.jsp.

Forbes. (2004, February 27). Christian Capitalism.

Gallagher, K. (2003). Assessment of current supply chain needs for the Christian retail industry. Evangelical Christian Publishers Association.

Garrett, L., Riess, J., & Tickle, P. (2003, August 4). CBA shows signs of struggle at annual convention. *Publishers Weekly*, p. 16.

GMA Media Relations. (2002). *Contemporary Christian and gospel music sales showing double-digit growth in spite of overall music industry declines* (press release). T. Whitehead, Gospel Music Association.

Hendershot, H., Ed. (2004). *Nickelodeon nation: The history, politics, and economics of America's only TV channel for kids.* New York: New York University Press.

Hogan-Albach, S. (1998, April 15). Religion's mass market. *Minneapolis Star Tribune*, p. 1.

Kapur, J. (1999). Out of control: Television and the transformation of childhood in late capitalism. In M. Kinder (Ed.), *Kids' media culture*, 122–136. Durham, NC: Duke University Press.

Kiesling, A. J. (2004, March 22). Religion publishing's black hole. *Publishers Weekly*, p. S10.

Leith, S. (2001, July 11). Spreading the gospel: Christian books hit the big time. *The Atlanta Journal-Constitution*, p. 1.

McChesney, R. W. (2000). The political economy of communication and the future of the field. *Media, Culture & Society* 22, 109–116.

McDannell, C. (1995). *Material Christianity: Religion and popular culture in America.* New Haven, CT: Yale University Press.

Murdock, G., & Golding, P. (1995). For a political economy of mass communications. In O. Boyd-Barrett and C. Newbold (Eds.), *Approaches to media: A reader*, 201–228. London: Arnold.

Nelson, M. (2003, November 10). How big is it, redux: Measuring the religion publishing industry is still an imprecise art. *Publishers Weekly*.

Porchlight Entertainment. (2003a). *Jay Jay the Jet Plane Lands on Canal+.* Retrieved March 24, 2004, from www.porchlight.com/press_details .php?.num=48.

Porchlight Entertainment. (2003b). *Porchlight Entertainment gives life to "Inspirational Baby" brand with inaugural launch of early development videos, DVDs, and books.* Retrieved March 24, 2004, from www.porchlight .com/press_release.php.

Porchlight Entertainment. (2004). About Jay Jay the Jet Plane. www.porchlight.com.

Seiter, E. (1995). *Sold separately: Parents and children in consumer culture.* New Brunswick, NJ: Rutgers University Press.

Smythe, D. (1957). *Structure and policy of electronic communication.* Urbana: University of Illinois Press.

Tommy Nelson. (2004). Jay Jay the Jet Plane. www.tommynelson.com.

Wilkin, P. (2001). *The political economy of global communication.* London: Pluto Press.

Wonderwings.com Entertainment. (2004). *Company.* Retrieved March 24, 2004, from www.wonderwings.com/company.html.

Zondervan. (2003). *Our growth.* Retrieved October 22, 2003, from www.zondervan.com/desk/about.asp?page=corpstats.

7

Selling the Gospel With Enthusiasm—or Just Selling?

Big Idea probably could have continued as an independent, primarily because we were acting for the most part as a production company, not a distribution company. Warner Brothers sold VeggieTales videos into Wal-Mart for us, and did quite well because the product was strong and because they sell more DVDs than any other company on Earth. So a good independent production company with a good product can almost always get good distribution. Self-distribution is another matter.

What has changed is the fact that any hit Christian product today hits Wal-Mart only 3 days after it hits Christian bookstores, so there's much less reason to go to a Christian bookstore. As a result, foot traffic in the CBA is way off, stores are closing, and the smaller audience going into Christian bookstores each month makes successfully launching a new entertainment project solely in the CBA much less likely. (Short of books, which have very little production cost and can afford to hang out in the CBA until someone notices them.)

So the VeggieTales model of growing a property in the CBA for a few years and then launching everywhere is unlikely to be repeated. Not that the CBA won't take it in, but that the CBA audience may now be too small to support the production cost of most entertainment projects.

On top of that, things like VeggieTales have raised quality expectations in the CBA, so new projects need to spend more to be accepted, further decreasing odds of success.

There needs to be a new model for developing Christian entertainment projects. That's one of the things I'm working on now.

—Phil Vischer (2004)

It is indisputable that *Veggie Tales* is a success and that it either changed the way Christian media operates or that it was the first sign that Christian media would have to change the way it operated. *Veggie Tales'* success is also clearly traceable to early evangelical outreach that used news media as a way of spreading not only notice of upcoming revivals, but also breathless accounts of the revivals themselves. This marriage between the media and Christian evangelicalism was nourished by both readership and attendance, respectively. In the nineteenth century, evangelicals decided to take the media into their own hands, and rather than solely trusting fellow Christians to reject mass media in favor of Bible reading, the evangelicals would create tracts and other printed materials that would provide "safe" entertainment and a means to lead others to salvation.

However, with the cultural push toward modernity and the social and political power of the mainline Protestant denominations, conservative evangelicalism was pushed to the side in the development of electronic mass media. The deal made between mainline denominations and the emerging radio networks virtually guaranteed the mainlines dominance on the airwaves and left little to no free time for the conservative evangelicals. Conservative evangelicalism or fundamentalism had already been pushed to the margins, most vividly in the 1925 Scopes trial, and the movement developed, out of the sight of most critics, refining its message to rejoin the national conversation (Harding,

1994). Some of that message was evident in the 2004 presidential election, and that market savvy can be traced in part to the movement's early days in radio.

Because conservative evangelicals had to pay for their radio time, they were forced to develop a message that was captivating enough that people would want to listen and to support the programming with donations (see Tona Hangen's excellent book *Redeeming the Dial: Radio, Religion, and Popular Culture in America* for further information). These broadcasts were clearly presented and engaging in delivery, they presented themselves squarely within acceptable evangelical discourse, and they made a compelling case for continued listening and support. These attributes meant the survival of this programming when mainline programming died after broadcasters were no longer required to provide free time. Conservative evangelicals had learned that a marriage with the market and corporate media could work to their benefit. The mass media could produce ungodly material that was dangerous, but it could also be used as a vehicle for reaching the masses with a message of salvation.

Televangelists learned this message so well that they began creating their own media organizations, and this method worked until the scandals of the late 1980s and until the cable and broadcast television industries became so competitive that it was increasingly difficult for independent religious channels to survive. *The 700 Club*, once a linchpin in evangelical programming, is now found primarily on a channel owned by the Walt Disney Company. But while traditional televangelism such as Joyce Meyer and newsmagazine-style programs such as *The 700 Club* don't garner much attention and have to be sought out by fans willing to get up early or buy full cable, a new generation of evangelical Christian media is making headlines.

Christian Cool?

It's not every day that the *New York Times* has a headline with "Christian Cool" in it (Leland, 2004a). But in 2004 major national and regional papers figured out that Christian media and para-phernalia had somehow become cool. Just as others have noted that young evangelicals want to have tangible evidence and re-minders of their faith (McDannell, 1995), American cultural in-dustries want to provide that tangible evidence. With the subhead "Christianity Becomes Cool," the *Wall Street Journal* found celebrities such as Madonna, Pamela Anderson, Ashton Kutcher, and Lara Flynn Boyle all wearing T-shirts with variants on "Jesus is my Homeboy" and "Mary is my Homegirl." The ac-tual spiritual proclivities of the celebrities seem to be irrelevant; Madonna's currently embracing Kabbalah, but wearing one's spirituality seems to be the thing, as long as one does it with cool graphics (Kang, 2004). It's also notable that the expected squirm-ing from devout evangelicals seems to be absent; perhaps they see this as a foothold in mass culture, despite the personal morality of the celebrities? Some interviewed for the *Journal* ar-ticle thought that the T-shirts, along with the new teen-oriented Bible magazine released by Thomas Nelson, might be a way for Christian teens to embrace their identity while still seeming cool. But others weren't so sure. "'Religion in its own way has become a brand, and right now it's hot,' says Jane Buckingham, presi-dent of Youth Intelligence, a New York trend-forecasting com-pany. But before too long, fashion-conscious teens and the retail buyers who cater to them may move on to the next thing, Ms. Buckingham warns" (Kang, 2004).

So some of these trends may just be tied to of-the-moment fashion, such as C28, the brand named for Colossians 2:8. Others say that these trends represent the yearning of youth for a more demanding, more personal identification with their faith. Like generations of youth before them, some teens are calling the re-ligion of their parents "dead" and demanding more of their own commitment. As one trend maker in the Christian media told the *New York Times*, "We don't want to show up on Sunday, sing two hymns, hear a sermon and go home. . . . The Bible says we're supposed to die for this thing. If I'm going to do that, this has to be worth something. Our generation wants a tangible experience of God who is there" (Leland, 2004a). And the cultural industries are more than happy to provide that tangible experience. The same media industry that provides Grand Theft Auto III also provides Catechumen, in which gamers "go through the catacombs of Rome to free a mentor and fellow Christians, converting the 'demon-possessed' Roman soldiers along the way" (Lin, 2003).

A Tangible Experience of God

This embrace of Christian cultural artifacts is different from both the nineteenth-century ambivalence about Christian novels noted by Moore and the personal and decorative use of material culture documented by McDannell. This embrace is personal and public and it's political and it's in your face. It's also being pushed not by devout Christian businesses, but by Urban Outfitters, Wal-Mart, and Warner Bros. The ambivalence about how publicly Christian Christian media should be is gone. Any ambivalence is now confined to those who are concerned about who controls that media and the growth of the industry; rank-and-file evangelicals seem, for the most part, happy about this marketing of their religion. It's a sign that mass culture has to pay attention to evangelicalism and the size of the evangelical Christian market. It's a sign that the evangelicals have won. The reward of hard work and diligence is economic success (Ferguson, 2003), but that success can also be seen as a sign of God's blessing.

In a sense, the bankruptcy of *Veggie Tales* can be seen as a sign of success. The demand for *Veggie Tales* products from both the Christian booksellers and the mass retail industry pushed the company over the edge. The company didn't go bankrupt because no one wanted the product or because the product was of poor quality; the company went bankrupt because everyone wanted, in the words of Cameron Strang, "a tangible experience of God." This meant licensing plush animals, books, toys, and videos and creating a feature-length film. This meant extending the Big Idea line beyond *Veggie Tales* into products to serve multiple markets, a la *Jay Jay the Jet Plane*. This meant creating a company that could stand alone for the sake of spiritual integrity but also had to be fully integrated with most aspects of the mass media industry. This was a lot to ask.

Some of the very factors that made *Veggie Tales* so successful also made its success very difficult to sustain. It had high production quality, it was fun and snappy, it had a devoted fan base, and it came on the market at just the right time. It also benefited from an integrated network of suppliers and distributors who could get the product on the shelves of the largest retailer in the world, where the series could find more fans. But this fast-moving train needs constant fuel, and, as Phil Vischer noted at the top of this section, every market entry has to be a hit. Wal-Mart clerks can't be counted on to build word of mouth the way that the local Christian bookstore owner can, and the local Christian bookstore is being pushed to the wall by the big box stores. The speed with which the media industry moves now means that media companies that are part of a consolidated media corporation will be able to take advantage of economies of scope and scale to keep product on the shelves and new product rolling along; this speed makes it hard for smaller organizations to even get going. In addition, now that the industry has discovered the profitability of the Christian market, that market can't return to obscurity.

What this means, at least to me, is that there is a split in the Christian media industry between the ministries and the companies. *Veggie Tales* will remain in production as a part of Classic Media and will probably maintain its Christian roots, although they will be marketed as "values" and "morals." And ministries such as Focus on the Family will remain in the marketplace with their alternative distribution and financing networks and their more aggressive display of Christian theology and politics. Both will continue to serve the evangelical market quite effectively because, in terms of the message for kids, the focus will remain on individual morals and personal piety, not on social issues that tend to be the purview of liberal Christians. But while *Veggie Tales* will begin and end with personal behavior, the Focus on the Family project includes a social agenda that builds upon that personal piety.

A Split in the Market and a Split in the Industry

To further illustrate the differences between Big Idea and Focus on the Family, let's consider the corporate structures of the two organizations. These structures support the two most popular Christian media products for kids, *Veggie Tales* and *Adventures in Odyssey*. In an attempt to see the relationship between the growth in their popularity, secularization theory, and the overall economic climate in which the Christian media operate, I looked at the core relationship between the core producer organization and any partners it might have. I theorized that media with a less exclusive message would tend to have a larger, more diverse network of partners than a media organization with a more exclusive message. This is not to say that certain kinds of organizations cause certain messages or vice versa, simply that they may be correlated. Big Idea, the producer of *Veggie Tales*, is identified as having the less exclusive message with its theme that God is loving and a focus on behavior-oriented goodness, such as obedience to parents, kindness to friends, and honesty. Alternatively, *Adventures in Odyssey*, created by Focus on the Family, is identified as being more exclusive, with an emphasis on Jesus and faith in God as the key themes. Focus on the Family reportedly rejected an opportunity to pick up the *Veggie Tales* series, saying that it wasn't very funny, and instead the distribution rights went to the larger Word Entertainment (Fargo, 1998).

Big Idea has nearly double the number of connections with outside organizations that Focus on the Family does (Borgatti, Everett, & Freeman, 1999). This should not be taken to mean that Big Idea is somehow superior, just more connected with outside organizations. Big Idea's profile is much more similar to Zondervan's in terms of market connectedness, and Zondervan started out in a similar way but is now owned by HarperCollins and, by extension, News Corporation. Another structural issue that bears mentioning is that of horizontal versus vertical integration. Focus on the Family maintains much of its own production, distribution, and marketing functions within its vertically integrated organization, thus enhancing its own control over all

aspects of its product. Big Idea, though, is much more horizon-
tally integrated, which enhances its opportunities for distribution but limits control. The variety of partners that Big Idea has
may also be one reason why Big Idea's *Veggie Tales* has a less exclusive, less demanding message—and thus appeals to a broad
audience in both Christian bookstores and Wal-Mart.

Of course Focus on the Family and Big Idea/*Veggie Tales* are
not the only organizations that are coping with a changing environment for religious media. PAX, as discussed in an earlier chapter, has been grappling with media concentration for years, and if
one looks at the schedule for a local PAX affiliate, the influence of
corporate ownership is clear. There's no religious programming in
traditional prime-time hours and little on the schedule at all. Joyce
Meyer and *CBN Newswatch* dominate religious-themed programming, but even that is relegated to the late evening. In addition,
Everland, an early partner with Big Idea in the distribution and
marketing of *Veggie Tales*, tried to find a new hit in the program
Threads in 2000, but now the DVDs seem to be out of print. Creative
Communications for the Parish, based in Missouri, has had a small
hit with its *Bed Bug Gang*, which does contain a Gospel message
but is open to both Catholic and Protestant church customers. This
series can also be found on the INSP cable network. What appears
to be happening in the religious media market is a "split between
sacred and secular," as noted with the differing markets for *Jay Jay
the Jet Plane* (Salamon, 2003).

This split creates additional pressure on organizations such
as Focus on the Family, who may be losing their lock on the
"family-friendly" market that isn't so particular about theology.
Also, as secular media producers become ever more adept at
market targeting and segmentation, these secular producers
may be able to slice away at all but the most devoted Focus
on the Family fans. This would encourage Focus on the Family
to increase its activity that builds its own organization, as has
already been seen with the activity to ban gay marriage and to
remind its faithful that the organization isn't just about media
production, but also about cultural action.

No doubt, parties on all sides of the secularization debate
can use this finding to spur their own argument, but for those in-

terested in the joint study of media and religion these findings point out a rich avenue of study: the role of the ever-concentrating media landscape in shaping the Christian message. Big Idea set out to be the Disney of the Christian family, and in terms of numbers of units sold, it has been successful. Focus on the Family sees its own mission as Christian evangelism and social action on a number of fronts, and to that end it may be successful as well, particularly if one looks at the social issues, such as abortion and gay marriage, on which Focus on the Family has weighed in.

Debates over secularization have pointed out that several kinds of religious adherence have developed, to either the benefit or detriment of religion in society. One is the preservation of more traditional religious orientation with an emphasis on strictness; the other is the orientation that emphasizes pluralism and allows for religion to permeate the culture without specific proscriptions. Given the current state of media concentration and the economic pressures created by a crowded media landscape and tight distribution networks, the Christian media organization, like many other media organizations, is finding itself encouraged to join with larger media players that might help in navigating the competitive marketplace. However, distributors and retailers seeking the largest possible audience should tend to prefer less exclusive messages, thus privileging the organization that produces those messages. In addition, the creator of the more exclusive messages might shun any compromises that might be required by participation in a broader network.

As American culture has become one of consumption and marketing it is natural that evangelical Christianity would have to contend with the same forces as the rest of the culture. So, has the dominance of the commercial culture meant the decline of a distinctive Christian culture, or has the sheer size and free-market friendliness of evangelical Christendom meant that the evangelical message has spread even further? In a recent radio interview (Tippett, 2004), Martin Marty said that evangelicalism has achieved dominance in the last century through its embrace of individual piety. This emphasis on personal choice fits well, says Marty, with a culture that is increasingly atomistic.

Evangelicals take seriously personal mandates about sexual morality, abortion, prayer, and group worship and see this as a largely personal matter. The messages in the most successful religious media also tend to hold to these issues rather than containing challenges to eliminate social problems such as poverty. The personal and family-based nature of evangelical faith is also supported by media choices that lend themselves well to individual, home-based use.

The success of religious media messages, and the embrace of these messages by corporate institutions (for profit reasons), means that these messages are more accepted, more welcomed, by the mainstream culture. The current mood is not one of keeping one's beliefs private—instead, American society expects its leaders and its citizens to be public about their faith. And, as we saw in the days following September 11, 2001, when a cross of metal girders emerged from the debris of the World Trade Center towers, Americans have maintained a fascination with the sacred, regardless of their personal faith.

With the interest of media corporations in religious products, it has become harder to define what is spiritual or religious. *Publishers Weekly* has already noted this in its attempts to define sales of religious titles, and booksellers are having difficulty in distinguishing between self-help, personal growth, religion, spirituality, and New Age. Should the latest Oprah-related book be shelved under self-help or spirituality? Stephen Covey: business or religion? This breadth of the market makes it harder to define, which makes it more exploitable by the industry, yet presents a greater challenge to the orthodox.

Individuals are also becoming more and more comfortable with public expressions of faith, as evidenced by Christian T-shirts, music gatherings, and, as reported in the *New York Times*, students from the U.S. Merchant Marine Academy at a worship gathering chanting, "We love Jesus, how about you?" (Leland, 2004b). Interestingly, one of the gathering's promoters said that what was selling was an accurate representation of what people need, spiritually. This is a dramatic claim: that spiritual needs in a culture can be best measured by sales figures.

References

Borgatti, S. P., Everett, M. G., & Freeman, L. C. (1999). UCINET 6.0 Version 1.00. Natick, MA: Analytic Technologies.

Fargo, C. (1998, October 25). Hot potatoes. *The State Journal-Register* (Springfield, IL).

Ferguson, N. (2003, June 8). Why America outpaces Europe (Clue: the God factor). *The New York Times.*

Harding, S. (1994). The born-again telescandals. In N. B. Dirks, G. Eley, & S. B. Ortner (Eds.), *Culture/power/history: A reader in contemporary social theory*, 539–556. Princeton, NJ: Princeton University Press.

Kang, S. (2004, May 5). Pop culture gets religion: Whether reverent or ironic, Christianity has become cool; "Homeboy" T's speak to teens. *The Wall Street Journal*, pp. B1–2.

Leland, J. (2004a, May 16). Christian cool and the new generation gap. *The New York Times.*

Leland, J. (2004b, April 17). Christian music's new wave caters to an audience of one. *The New York Times*, p. A8.

Lin, E. (2003, September 16). Spiritually profitable gaming. *Forbes*, www.forbes.com.

McDannell, C. (1995). *Material Christianity: Religion and popular culture in America*. New Haven, CT: Yale University Press.

Salamon, J. (2003, December 27). Marketing strategy splits the sacred and the secular. *New York Times.*

Tippett, K. (Writer). (2004). America's changing religious landscape. *Speaking of Faith.* [Radio]. American Public Media.

Vischer, P. (2004). E-mail correspondence with author.

Index

About the Author

Hillary Warren is Assistant Professor of Communication at Otterbein College in Westerville, Ohio. She is on the editorial board of the *Journal of Media and Religion*, head of the Religion and Media Interest Group of the Association for Education in Journalism and Mass Communication, and writes on religion and media for several academic journals. A former journalist, Warren teaches courses on media law, news writing, and reporting.